Driving ROI

A summarized venture into

Storytelling, Listening, and Measuring

John E. Murray, III

Driving ROI. Copyright © 2007 by John E. Murray, III.

Printed and bound in the United States of America. All rights reserved. No part of this book may be reproduced in any form or by any electronic or mechanical means including information storage and retrieval systems without permission in writing from the author, John E. Murray, III, except by a reviewer, who may quote brief passages in a review.

LC Control No.: 2007934026

Murray, John E.

Driving Roi : a summarized venture into storytelling, listening, and measuring / John E. Murray, III.

p. cm.

ISBN-13: 978-0-9794451-0-1 (pbk.)

ISBN-10: 09794451-0-8 (pbk.)

For permission or other resources, please visit:

www.storyinstitute.com or send an email to JohnEMurrayIII@storyinstitute.com

To my wife, Teri, who enriches
my timeless tales
through every meandering path

Contents

Starting Up

Driving Home

Resources & Tools for Driving ROI

Prelude

When tales do we tell,

Inside, meaning must dwell.

While ideas circle, collide, and swirl,

To select one insightful pearl,

We lightly linger and weave

Through intensities each believe.

Excitement mounts until the expected end,

As each delicate page we do bend.

In between can be found,

Delightful descriptions and rich details abound.

A truly timeless tale found within

Answers perfectly how and where to begin.

Starting UP...

ROI is always about return-on-investment...right?

Who determines the return? The executives? The managers? The trainers? The marketing team? The front-line staff? All of these together?

What classifies as the investment? The labor? The time? The material? The technology? The creative thoughts? All of them together?

Even if we answer all of these questions, we still have to determine whether we are going to calculate the arithmetic or logarithmic return...Right?

Traditional return-on-investment calculations are as numerous as the training programs they represent. Before we venture down the path of choosing the "right-fit" formula, we must consider our audience. Ask yourself, what is driving their ROI.

We need to understand where we fit within the ROI path. We need to understand our role and be prepared to deliver against expectations other than our own. We may even be the bridge between the Operations and Training or the Executives and the Operations. Either way, by understanding what drives R.O.I., we are better able to communicate and positively impact the organization...After all, this is what we all desire, a bigger impact for the organization...Right?

Throughout this venture, we will explore some unique ways in which executives, training teams, operators, and marketing teams align their efforts around what they define as excellence in action. Many may disagree with the terms. Many more may have other representations for what each letter represents. All dialogue helps understand the direction each individual takes when establishing their own ROI.

We will need to understand the mindset and goals of the Executives if you are in Training or Operations. We will need to address the needs of the Operations if you are an Executive or part of the Training Team. And, we will need to appreciate the intricacies and support the complexities of Training if we are an Executive or in Operations.

We will need to create mechanisms and build an integrated listening post for our brand, our product, and our organization. Feedback hubs influence strategy and drive learning results. Learning results will influence operational success. Operational success has an impact on both the customer and business as marketing plans, key messages, and storylines merge to establish a lasting and loyal relationship with our customers, vendors, and partners.

Driving ROI

As you complete the surveys and read the stories that follow, keep asking what drives your R.O.I. There are no right or wrong answers to the surveys, only alternative ways of looking at a similar picture. Not necessarily the same picture, rather a similar one. Read each section, no matter what you define as your role as you may find overlaps within your area of responsibility and connections to drive a different ROI. In the end, remember to share each point, each piece of your scope with your partners, peers, and leaders. This will create a unified level of excellence.

Executive ROI

Definition:
Refine Goals, Offer Assistance, Initiate Change

Key to Success: Communicate

Please indicate the extent to which you agree with each of the statements below:

Question	Strongly Agree	Agree	Sometimes Agree/ Sometimes Disagree	Disagree	Strongly Disagree
Profits measure the success of a company.	O	O	O	O	O
Minimizing labor maximizes efficiency.	O	O	O	O	O
Managing for results produces peak performance.	O	O	O	O	O
Engaging in the daily operations demonstrates understanding and appreciation of frontline staff responsibilities.	O	O	O	O	O
Training improves performance.	O	O	O	O	O

Executive Focus...

As an executive, your focus is to get the most out of the least. Your goal is to succeed in every aspect of your business. Your key to achieving a positive return on investment is to communicate, communicate, communicate.

You are in and out of meetings every moment of every day. You barely have time to sit at your desk, let alone a training class. You are the strategy…You are the vision. The goals need to be set and refined. Since you are not the content expert, you need to trust your operators, your trainers, your teams to deliver on the expectations you set.

If you plan on being successful over the long-term, you need to be willing to refine your goals as you gain more knowledge. As plans are implemented that reinforce the strategy, you will need to offer your assistance. You also should be the first to initiate change, remembering to check in with all levels of staff as the process is rolled out and behaviors are impacted. By having a face in the organization, you will help the people travel along the varied change management paths they decide to follow. Paths, each of us follow every day, sometimes on our way home…

Chapter One – Executive ROI

Driving ROI:

You are driving home from the office. You begin thinking about what will erupt when you announce the implementation of the new software that is being brought in "to make things "easier" in efforts to meet our financial goals while streamlining the processes for the operations"…at least that is what the IT report indicated…training will have two weeks after acceptance testing to develop and deliver training to your staff of 1500.

You are just about to pick up your cell phone to check your voicemail, when you see the taillights brighten on the car in front of you. You step on your brake pedal and slow down with the rest of traffic. You remember hearing sirens when you left the office and believe an accident is somewhere on this road.

You look around for a way out. The side streets here don't cross any of the major streets that you need to get home, but they may get you further along this road and out of the traffic. You turn your wheel slightly to the right when traffic moves forward. You decide to forgo the side streets and move with traffic.

You move forward only halfway down the block when the traffic stops again. You will have to wait to take any other route…

Driving ROI

Or, will you? You could turn around, head back to your office, and wait until the traffic subsides.

You turn your wheel slightly to the left. Traffic moves forward again. You decide to go a little further and flow with the others. You move to the next side street, but the traffic stops there. Your patience is wearing thin and you need to figure out a solution for communicating the implementation plan tomorrow. You turn right down the next side street, hoping to get ahead of these other cars and just keep moving.

As you complete your turn, you notice three other cars behind you. "Huh, copycats," you think aloud. You travel about five blocks, the other cars are still in view. On the sixth street, you decide to make your way back to the main thoroughfare and turn left. As you complete your turn, you realize that many others had the same idea.

You decide to turn around and try another street. This time, only one car follows. At the end of each block, you slow down and check the streets before you turn. Finally, you find a path that has only two cars. You turn down that road. You check your rear-view mirror and realize the other car must have turned down another street.

Chapter One – Executive ROI

You decide to turn on your radio to see if there is any information about the situation. As you get closer to the other cars, the babbling from the news station mentions a fire hydrant burst and flooding on the roadway...and under the two cars in front of you. You slowed down enough to hit the end of the quickly expanding pool at a stop.

You back and begin to turn around again. If only you had listened to the radio, if only you had stayed on the path you set, if only you had not left the office so early...if only...

These situations happen. Have they happened to you? Did you stay the path? Did you turn around? Did you just pull off on a side street and make some calls? We all seem to be rushing for a quicker way home, a quicker return on investment. However, we rarely receive the return we wish.

In fact, we may waste time by trying different paths. Others may follow. We may exhaust more money in labor or invest in one technology to "fix" another. It's like turning down a side street with a larger back-up of cars then the one you tried to escape.
We may eventually need to revert to the original path because we reached a point of negative return so large that it overshadowed and even flooded the original investment.

Throughout the entire scenario, we rarely thought about getting home. However, we did think about the meeting the next day and the getting ahead of the other cars. If we can't remind ourselves of the path or the vision, who will remind the organization?

Vision is not always 20/20...

Sometimes, it is clouded by heights

no one intended to reach

since the beginning...

As the executive, as the vision and strategy, you need to set and refine goals, offer assistance, and initiate change, especially as new projects are rolled out, especially as you reflect on the questions asked at the beginning of the chapter.

Survey in Motion:

Profits are numbers, not measurements...

The excess of money gained over the amount of money spent. Does that sound like success to you?

Profits may demonstrate good business decisions, such as setting the price of an item higher than your costs. Profits may even allow organizations to invest in additional resources.

Profits can not tell you what the customers think of a product. Profits can not tell you how well co-workers partner. Profits can not tell you if training was worth the labor you invested in it. Profits, especially in the short-term, can not push the company into long-term equilibrium.

Communicating your vision continuously and being open to refining your goals will allow your organization to reach higher levels of success.

Efficiency is achieved through maximizing opportunities...

Minimizing labor, especially if it is done by shortening training, can end up costing your organization more money than it saves. If you focus on the opportunities, you may find a way to shorten the initial training, but you will need to plan for reinforcement somewhere around 20 to 30 days out. If you do not, the knowledge gained will slowly decline. At that point, you may be faced with re-training your entire staff. This usually occurs about 6 months later. As long as you plan on being in a different role before that mark, you can afford the quick wins.

Refining goals rears its ugly head again. You should be open to listening to your operators and your training team as they collect satisfaction, knowledge, and application assessments. Understanding the results can realign the organization to the goals you set.

Leading people encourages peak performance...

As an executive, you lead the organization and offer assistance to others on how to lead their teams. If you involve yourself in the management of things, results will be negative. Someone has to keep the focus on a higher strategy. Someone has to ground the organization on what success looks like.

By offering assistance to your organization at various points, and demonstrating how to lead, especially in times of change, you commit to the success of the project and your organization. You also demonstrate that you want continuous ROI, not just one big enough to build your own career.

Chapter One – Executive ROI

Driving for results is good if you have a purpose. Negative reinforcement of training by penalizing those that "fail" assessments instead of understanding where gaps lie, will negatively impact results, especially short-term results. Offer opportunities to demonstrate knowledge and application. Offer positive reinforcement through recognition for high levels of application. By leading through change, you can manage your return more thoroughly.

Listening to and trusting employees expresses understanding and appreciation...

How many times have you heard, "they" don't know what we do...or, "they" couldn't do our job...or even, "they" need to do our job, then "they'll" understand. Guess who the "they" is...If you said, you, the executive, you are correct. It is any decision-maker, but executives get the most of this responsibility.

Many executives have either been there, done that, or feel it is not their place to do the work of their staff. That attitude, like it or not, is negative and will negatively impact the organization. The results can be positive though. Listen to your employees and trust that they know their job. In fact, they possess more knowledge about their roles than you. Communicate your thoughts about the direction of the company, but listen to the experts. Remember, increasing knowledge enhances application. This leads to a more positive return on your investment.

Driving ROI

As an executive, you should stay focused on the vision. The more you become involved in the day-to-day activities of your organization, the further from your vision will your organization move. The reason for this is quite simple. If you engage in the daily operations, there is no one to remind the teams why they are working so hard...why the content of the training is important...and why it is significant to transition knowledge into application.

> **Remembering is only painful if we choose to forget first...**

People improve performance...

Training allows an organization to share knowledge. It doesn't impact performance directly. Rather, it allows people in the organization to grow and use their understanding to increase their application. This application should be based on the strategy and direction of the organization.

Chapter One – Executive ROI

This is where executives can make the most impact on an organization, initiate change on the thought process of a company. The traditional "business" thought is that people attend training where satisfaction and knowledge is measured initially. Application is measured 60-90 days afterwards. ROI can be shown beyond that point. There is usually something missing in between satisfaction and knowledge measurements and application calculations…the missing item is reinforcement.

Usage is not enough to reinforce the material. The leadership of an organization needs to remind everyone of the goals within their projects. This is a change in thought process. In fact, this transforms training into learning. Training is usually an event or series of events with a finite timeline. Learning, however, is continuous.

> **Planning for a tomorrow that never arrives makes today much busier, but we learn more through each experience…**

Driving ROI

Encourage continuous interaction between your training staff and your operations. In order for your operations teams to deliver, the training team needs to listen after the formal event is complete. Communicate to your operators the expectations on delivery. Communicate to your training teams the gaps that occur after training. This gap usually occurs within 20 and 45 days after the initial training event, and again, every 3 months thereafter. This becomes a continuous learning process and the return can be sustained past 90 days. Simple interactions between the groups and yourself can help avoid additional large training events in the future.

> **We all learn from our successes,**
>
> **But we excel further from our failures...**

ROI in Action:

One method of encouraging interaction is setting the base for an integrated listening post with an employee feedback hub. Employee satisfaction surveys, recognition programs, and idea programs make up a successful base. Your feedback hub will provide opportunities for your training team to connect learning objectives to business objectives.

Integrated Listening Post – Strategic Module

Employee
Satisfaction Surveys
Recognition Programs
Idea Programs

Training ROI

Definition:
Recognize Impact, Organize Delivery, Integrate Learning

Key to Success: Listen

Please indicate the extent to which you agree with each of the statements below:

Question	Strongly Agree	Agree	Sometimes Agree/ Sometimes Disagree	Disagree	Strongly Disagree
A well-designed training class, has the primary impact to application.	O	O	O	O	O
Aligning training objectives to business objectives ensures the training will be successful.	O	O	O	O	O
Constantly modifying training based on satisfaction results leads to increased knowledge.	O	O	O	O	O
Proper needs assessments create optimal training delivery methods that impact application results.	O	O	O	O	O
Knowledge and skill assessments measure how effectively content is trained within a learning event.	O	O	O	O	O

Chapter Two – Training ROI

Training Focus...

As a member of the training team, your responsibility is to share knowledge with individuals, groups, and organizations. Your goal is to encourage satisfaction so that the audience learns the content to the extent that they apply it. Your key to increasing application so that it positively impacts an organization's return on investment is to listen, listen, listen.

You design and deliver content to the masses. You are stretched so far, you can't guarantee that all of the content is within each class let alone that it will be used. Everything becomes your issue. If the staff is not performing, you need to develop more training. If the phone lines or intranet stop working, you need to train another method of communication. It never stops. You are the experts even though you rarely apply the content outside of the classroom or test environment.

If your team plans on being successful in transferring learning to behavior, you will need to recognize the impact of how you train and organize the delivery of these events so that learning is integrated in the initial approach and there is continuous reinforcement. Take a step back from training and assist the organization in the learning process. Where training is usually a single or series of events, learning contains continuous activities. Learning also allows for reinforcement. Plan for what your participants will forget.

This is easily recognized through Level 2, knowledge assessments, and listening to your operation partners. With the gaps in knowledge shown in the Level 2 evaluations added to the feedback from your clients, you can use adult-learning techniques to bridge those gaps while building upon the strengths of previous learning events. Bridges that can be built and crossed when we choose…

Driving ROI:

You are on the expressway headed into work for another long day of training. You hope to get in early this morning to prep for the class this afternoon. This class will be full of front-line employees who are learning the new system being brought in "to make things "easier" in efforts to meet our financial goals"…

Traffic slows to a crawl just as you near the ramp to the toll road. Without hesitating, you merge onto the ramp. You've seen traffic back up on this road before and know that it adds an extra 20 minutes to your commute if you stay on the original path that is.

Traffic is clipping along at a nice pace even as you near the first toll. You slow down and look for some change on the dash or the cup holders. You do not seem to find any coins, so you reach into your pocket, and take out a couple of dollar bills. As you near the booth, you realize that you are in the "exact change" lane and need to merge. You do so, but cut in front of a couple other cars. One honks at you.

Chapter Two – Training ROI

You pay the toll, thank the collector, and begin accelerating into the funnel of lanes. There are only two lanes and five booths with cars exiting at all points. You speed up and slow down with similar motions and manage to make your way into the flow of traffic.

The cars pick up speed and so do you. You can exit at the next ramp and take the streets from there. However, you choose to travel one more exit and backtrack a little as planned.

You hit rumble strips again and remember the second toll. You take the second dollar out of your pocket, slow down, and roll down your window. You pay the second toll, which is slightly more than the first, and begin the race for the lanes again. You can't speed up too much since the exit for which you were waiting is right on the other side of the toll booths.

Now, the easy part, backtracking through the side streets and getting into work…

Expressways and toll roads are great ways to reach your destination. We pay for expressways through our taxes. Toll roads, however, have various collection points to remind you of the convenience of using them…yet, you also pay taxes that support the same materials for the toll roads. Would you have thought about the detour? Would you have exited a little earlier? Would you have gone in early that day instead?

Driving ROI

We all may have that first and possible second detour already planned within our training. We may even decide to go out of our way to add content that has little or no connections to the original scope. We do this because someone said, "we also have to train this topic with the new system because we don't have any other time to train it."

Interesting, we don't have time to train that topic any other time, but we will pay the price of putting too much into the one training event we are able to schedule right now. In fact, this would be similar to the multiple cars merging into a couple of lanes. While not impossible, others have to speed up or slow down for things to fit together and flow smoothly.

As a training team, your focus needs to remain on the design and delivery of training that has avenues of reinforcement. Without reinforcement, you will pay for the labor, but not reap the application results. Most technical skills are lost within 20-30 days after training if they are not used in the same way they were trained. Most soft skills become dormant if someone doesn't remind the learners of the reason why they attended a learning event on specific topics within 5 – 10 days. As adults, we assume we know the softskills even before the class since we know the definitions. Reinforcement of the class details becomes important if we wish the material to be applied in a particular way.

Chapter Two – Training ROI

In order to accomplish all of the tasks that land on your plate, you need to remember to recognize the impact of the content and the training itself, organize the delivery for the initial class and the continuous learning events afterwards, reinforcing the content, and integrate learning with previous training sessions to show value and provide your learners with a solid base of understanding before and during application.

> **Adults learn as adults...**
>
> **However, they apply knowledge as a professional...**
>
> **It is important to provide translation**
>
> **Somewhere along the way...**

Survey in Motion:

Reinforcement provides a primary impact to application…

The number one reason why training fails is that it is not supported by the leaders after it is delivered. The number one reason learning fails is that it is not reinforced. Both are similar, yet different in their distinct ways.

Leaders who choose not to reiterate the importance of a training event push the trainees further away from the intent of the training class. The mindset of the participant shifts to, "well, if my manager doesn't know about the class, why should I?" Negativity fosters negativity. If you choose, or your organization chooses, to have training events, then your leaders should attend the training as well. The success of the initial program is always on the training team. However, the long-term impact is felt more in the operations. By recognizing the impact of training, you will need to set a transition point so that your partners in the operations and support areas can pick up where you left off. They will be significantly challenged to do this if they do not have an idea about what was learned within the training. The higher up you go in the organization, the broader your view.

Leaders who choose not to make the content a part of their every day interactions with their staff will assist in the decay of the learning process. Negativity plays a small role here, but lack of usage, lack of interest, and higher levels of priority push out the content of a learning event. The success of a continuous learning process is always on training and development. As training professionals, we need to organize delivery effectively and provide job-aids or reminders at various times after the training. The reinforcement tools provide leaders with opportunities to talk about and direct their staff toward growing from a learning experience rather than just attending a class.

People ensure learning will be successful...

By aligning your training objectives to business objectives, you help fill gaps in content from a learning perspective. You can conduct multiple needs assessments and analyze the data until the cows come home...however, since most live in a city environment now, you may be analyzing an awful long time. You can even make sure the content aligns proportionally to the greatest and least need of your organization. This still will not ensure success. It only helps it along.

> **Learning is a funny thing...**
> **It is only successful when a learner**
> **Decides to become involved in the process...**

Learning is a challenging task and it takes people to make it work well. Sure, you can have online, web-based, PDA learning events, but someone, somewhere, has to put the event together. An even greater number of people are needed to hold things in place after participants engage in the learning. As adults, we have to link some importance to content before it replaces something else in our short-term or long-term memory. People, whether they are leaders, trainers, or executives, need to connect the dots for us after we attend a learning event by talking about how it relates to our everyday work.

We can look toward measurements to help integrate the learning experiences. Through satisfaction measurements, we are able to understand what marketing of the training needs to take place for the next group. Through knowledge assessments, we are able to revise or reinvent how content is delivered to a group after they attend the initial training so that we can build off of it. With Level 3 surveys, we can recognize the impact of our efforts and minimize the effect of work-arounds or lack of focus on our ROI.

> **Measuring what is not applied creates more work for those who are measuring...**

Chapter Two – Training ROI

Satisfaction results are summary points…

After a training class is complete, the first thing we need to do is examine the satisfaction surveys…or, at least that is what so many training professionals do. You may skip to the end and read the comments. Or, look at one particular question or set of questions to determine if your training was successful. This would be a daunting task for even the most mathematical minded among us.

Unless you can calculate correlations and build scattergrams in your head, understanding the success of your training based on quick glances at pieces of paper will probably not occur. What does happen, however, is that we create an imaginary summary and decide to change our approach and sometimes, even modify the content for the next class. This can be hazardous to your training and driving your positive ROI.

Remember to recognize the impact of your approach, delivery, and design. If training is changed constantly and the content shifts, you will lose the largest group of reinforcement you may have…the learners themselves. You may also create more work for yourself, as the job-aids will need to be different from class 1 to class 20. It is a good idea to conduct pilot classes and change content from there. Remember though to bring back those people when the final class structure is set. Every time you change, you have to determine what influenced the change. Basic statistics can help with this. However, you will need to decide when to use it. Is it in the revision of the training for a new hire class? Or, is it within your reinforcement plan? The goal is to minimize impact and maximize application in this situation.

Optimal learning comes in different formats...

Needs assessments are almost a necessity these days in any training environment. Designers, analysts, and leaders can devise a plan to hold dialogue sessions, focus groups, or focused dialogues with specific questions around the topic at hand. This same group may also align the gaps identified within these sessions to the goals of the organization. They will even develop a class, a tool, or an event to address these gaps.

However, in order for optimal learning to occur, different formats must be created. Using the expertise of an instructional designer and possibly an analyst, you can determine which format is right for the initial training and what may be a better fit for follow-up sessions. You may determine that there are too many questions to be answered with an online resource and start with a classroom setting. However, as your population begins applying the learning, you can introduce
a web-based class for reinforcement with various checks for understanding built into the tool.

Integrating a gap analysis approach into your delivery methods will help increase your ROI through connections made within the learning itself. This shows the importance of the events and the organization's investment in the people rather than the product, service, or system. Integrated learning indicates an investment itself rather than a point in time.

> **Sometimes, when alignment is out of sorts, it creates all sorts of alternate sometimes...**

Assessments measure knowledge of learners...

Knowledge and skill assessments should be based on the learning objectives for the class. The questions should be distributed proportionally across the learning objectives based on the percentage of content for each objective. The learning objectives themselves are best aligned with business objectives to determine the importance and priority of focus. The business objectives will need to be identified and developed prior to creating learning objectives.

Driving ROI

Knowledge and skill assessments are a good source to measure what knowledge the participants have when they leave the learning environment. However, unless you conduct a pre-assessment, it can be difficult to determine if they learned it from the training or enter the class with the knowledge. Participants may not communicate their knowledge effectively in a pre-assessment even if they know the content, especially if the questions still need to be tested for construct (can the knowledge be used effectively) and criteria-related (is the knowledge being used by top performers) validity.

Application evaluations become more difficult when you try to educate a group who might be familiar with the content. How do you know when behaviors stem from a class or learning event you devised? How do you know that your content didn't trigger an approach participants learned at an earlier stage in their careers? At times, we may not know if someone's past experience aided him/her in understanding material better. All this should be taken into consideration before a level of competency, application, and ROI are calculated and set.

ROI in Action:

An integrated listening post helps set and maintain our learning environment. If we tie in what employees are saying to leaders and reinforce the messages within a learning environment, they will be more satisfied. If they are more satisfied, they will learn and apply more.

Integrated Listening Post – Learning Module

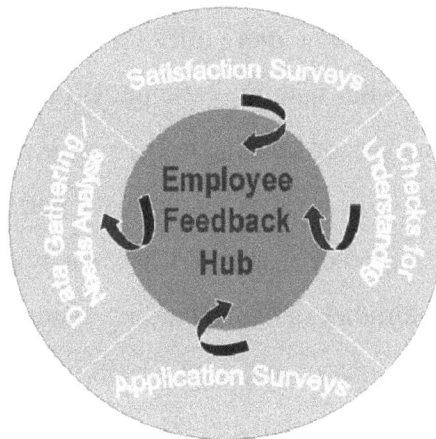

Operations & Support ROI

Definition:
Reinforce Content, Operate Efficiently, Increase Awareness

Key to Success: Deliver

Please indicate the extent to which you agree with each of the statements below:

Question	Strongly Agree	Agree	Sometimes Agree/ Sometimes Disagree	Disagree	Strongly Disagree
Serving more customers will increase our profits and reputation.	O	O	O	O	O
Since the members of the training team are experts in content, it is good to use them when the operations are short-staffed.	O	O	O	O	O
Peak productivity is achieved quicker if everyone accepts change when it is first communicated.	O	O	O	O	O
Learning is important, but on-the-job training is more effective in maintaining behavior.	O	O	O	O	O
Supporting decisions once they are made is always in the best interest of the company.	O	O	O	O	O

Chapter Three – Operations & Support ROI

Operations & Support Focus…

As a member of the operations and support teams, your primary responsibilities are to deliver on the expectations of executives and reinforce content from the training team. You are given a limited amount of resources to produce efficient and high-impact results for the entire organization. You have the burden of goal fulfillment. Your key to exceeding expectations is deliver, deliver, deliver.

Remember, you are not alone through this enormous process. Your executives, training, and marketing partners are there to provide you and the organization with strategic direction and tools. Focus on delivering and leading your teams. Focus on providing feedback to your executives and training partners as you all work toward a common goal of obtaining and maintaining a positive return on investment.

Reinforcing the content from training translates into understanding the impact of the training. Be the first to attend the events, possibly even alongside your staff. Ask your training partners to develop a class that will assist you in managing the change, new learning, or reinforcement process. However, don't miss the opportunity to learn. Or, try to learn the details at the extensive level that your staff will be learning them.

Leading teams within operations doesn't mean that you can do the job of your staff all the time. In fact, since you will not be doing their job enough, you are going to forget those details after a short while. It does mean, however, that you can assist when needed. It means that you know the systems and terms well enough to talk with your employees and customers. It means that you can troubleshoot if something in the process breaks or slows down...

Managers organize things...

Leaders inspire people...

Driving ROI:

You are driving to your favorite lunch place. You have a small amount of time before you have to be back in the office. That is, since you just implemented the new system that is meant "to make things "easier"... while streamlining the processes for the operations"...

The location is not too far away, so you guess there will be enough time... you forgot, however, to add gas to your car. So, a gas station is expected sooner than lunch. You think of where the next station may be, and realize that none are on this side of the street.

Chapter Three – Operations & Support ROI

As you near the next light, a gas station comes into sight on the far left. You merge into the turn lane, hoping to catch an arrow. There is no one in front of you. Within seconds, the main light turns green, no arrow. You look around and see a sign next to the light "turn on arrow or green." You inch out into the intersection and wait until the line of cars from the other side clear enough for you to make your turn and pull into the station.

You circle the lot once and pull up next to a pump. You turn the car off, take the keys out of the ignition, and unlatch your seat belt. Just as you reach for your door handle, you notice plastic bags over the nozzles and a sign that says, "Out of Order." So, you buckle up, insert your keys and turn the ignition…nothing. You look at the gas gage and hope that it wasn't that bad…the needle is still a little above the red line, so you try it again. This time, the car starts.

You put it in gear and circle the pumps again for any available space. This time, looking for the plastic bags before stopping. You notice someone pulling out and creep in behind him. He inches forward slightly and stops. Your car begins to putter a little, the engine revs, and you wait…

The car in front of you pulls forward and out. You glide into the spot. You quickly put the car in park, turn it off, and unlatch your seat belt again. You look around for any signs. Nothing. You get out of your car and proceed to go through the convenience added procedures of putting gas in your car. The handle clicks and you are done. You take your receipt, get back in your car, and go through the same ritual you do every time you enter your vehicle. You pause for a moment before you turn the ignition and hope the problem was just the low gas tank. You hear the roar and hum of the engine. You breathe a sigh of relief and shift into drive.

Just as you pull out of the station, you glance at the clock on the bank across the street. The time has dwindled down too far for you to make it to lunch and back as quickly as you would have liked. You notice a fast-food place next to the gas station and decide to go through the drive-thru and eat on your way back...

We can plan our time. We can plan our course. The part that we can not plan is what others control, such as the lights, traffic, or where gas stations are placed. We know that a car needs gasoline to function. But, how often do we let that little light come on before we fill up again? How often do we push our means of transportation to its extreme? When was the last time you had the oil changed? Or, the tire pressure checked?

Chapter Three – Operations & Support ROI

We can roll out a new system to help the organization and plan how it will be used. However, if we only roll out the system and don't check in with the users, reinforcing the importance and content, the money invested in the system will be a loss. By waiting until you are almost out of gas, or your employees are out of enthusiasm, you lose momentum…you lose productivity…you lose time. The more time you lose, the more you spend in labor. The more you spend in labor, the lower your return on investment.

In order to maximize your return on investment, attention should be paid to reinforcing content from training and sharing the importance of change. Operating efficiently involves listening and adapting before morale is impacted. Your listening, helps increase awareness of the various aspects of a project and reminds your staff why the organization has made changes. Increasing awareness also flows the other way. While listening to your teams, you should share their solutions and concerns with your leaders in order to influence continual growth.

> **Training fails when it is not supported…**
> **Learning fails when it is not reinforced…**

Survey in Motion:

Customer satisfaction is key to increased profits...

You can serve customers through marketing, sales, and returns. Just because you tell people about your company, doesn't mean that they will purchase your items or services. Just because your company sells products or services, doesn't mean your clients will not return the item itself, or ask for their money to be returned. Ideally, the more customers that purchase your products, the higher your profits should climb. Higher sales, however, do not always equal customer satisfaction.

If you focus on delivering quality to your customers, they will help increase your profits. Word-of-mouth marketing is worth more than a 30 second spot in any major sporting event. In order to understand what your customers need, you should listen to your teams and reinforce their listening skills. When you listen to them, it demonstrates a positive behavior and encourages your team to do the same for the customers. These comments should be shared with your partners in training and marketing.

Chapter Three – Operations & Support ROI

Trainers are expert trainers....

Trainers know the content of their training enough to apply it effectively. They can tell you or any member of your staff why you conduct one process before another. Trainers can demonstrate the ideal patterns of usage for the content they train. They can also help reinforce the messages of the organization with you.

However, trainers are experts in training and learning. If you pull them to "help" the customers, who is helping your staff? Who is helping you? Customers always come first. However, by focusing on the numbers rather than the quality, you will negatively impact your customer satisfaction in the long run. Busy periods are the best times for the trainers and leaders to spend time with the staff to listen and learn about the flow of the process. Using your trainers to reinforce the content of training and how it connects to the business objectives and marketing plan can help you operate more efficiently. You build the skillset of your staff so that they can handle more customers, more effectively.

If you use trainers to act as expert front-line staff, you will watch the skills of the actual front-line staff decline and your customer satisfaction level out, and even begin to dip over time. You will also see your training quality decline over an even longer time as your trainers become burned out. They will not consider themselves qualified trainers. They will, however, feel like glorified front-line staff. For those who enjoy the learning process, this will not be enough. Eventually, you will lose your best trainers because you didn't respect them and the skills they bring. Remember, if you are not respecting your staff and your partners, your customers will eventually feel the same way.

> ## Expertise is a funny creature...
> ## it often disappears when another like beast
> ## enters the lair...

Diversity enables peak performance...

Change is always a personal thing. We can say that we accept the change within an organization, but the extreme to which we accept it always varies. Just look at any change cycle model if you question this. Each will show you that there are steps one goes through from intrusion/loss to integration/acceptance. We all start at different places along the path to acceptance. However, it is the reinforcement of the message that will lead us to a more positive environment.

If everyone went through change the same way, we would have very little diversity. Without diversity in actions and thoughts, we would be a rather boring company. We would not be able to market our products well since we would only understand our way, which may be different from what our customers prefer. We would not be able to troubleshoot problems because everyone would come up with the same ideas, the same ones that do not work now. If we all accepted the changes in the same way, we would not be able to grow as a company and as individuals. We would stay where we are personally and professionally.

While supporting an idea or direction is good business sense, supplying alternatives to the approach and offering suggestions for improvements should be welcomed from all levels of the staff. It would make it extremely difficult for marketing to sell a product or service if they don't know what the customers are saying about our current offerings. It would make it very challenging to lead a team without a focus, and you can not develop a focus unless you listen and communicate.

> **Growing inward before looking outward**
> **Helps others realize successes together...**

Driving ROI

Reinforcing learning is the most important component to changing behavior...

On-the-job training and application is essential to understanding what needs to be accomplished for a role. In fact, adults learn effectively by doing. With on-the-job training, a skilled person shares his/her knowledge with an unskilled person within certain responsibilities. The results of this situation are positive in the short-term only if the person who shares the knowledge is available to consistently answer questions about the tasks needed to be accomplished.

As a leader, you will need to understand the resources available to you and your team. You will need to remind them of the importance of their tasks. You will need to reinforce the content within their training. Work with training and/or your communications teams to create job-aids or key messages to share with your staff at planned intervals after the initial training takes place. These resources should center on gaps identified in knowledge and skill assessments as well as application assessments.

This is the importance of each step within the evaluation process. Take part in and encourage your team to take part in all aspects of the measurement process. By supplying information to the training and marketing teams as well as your executives, your job becomes easier. The executives will be able to adjust their expectations. The training team will be able to work on continuous learning projects rather than focusing on the get-them-in, get-them-out philosophy. The marketing team can share more of the story or reinforce the key messages about the item. This helps increase knowledge and enables you to lead your team rather than managing resources.

> ## Agreement, if stated in a vacuum, gets whirled around and dusty just like the rest of the debris..

Improving on decisions is best for the company...

Leaders within an organization make decisions everyday, some good, some questionable. You are always told that if you do not support a decision once it is made, you are not a "team player." If you are not considered a "team player," your opportunities within the organization may decrease. It is OK to have an opinion, really. It is how you choose to share your opinion that becomes the challenge.

Deliver on the decision that has already been made, and do so to the best of your ability. Share your solution-oriented feedback. Increase awareness of the vision and importance of your organization with your teams and peers. Set the example. Understand that the solution you are supporting is just the first step in a successful business.

Executives or decision-makers in organizations may not have enough time or even enough information to plan the full implementation of a project. This is your opportunity to take ownership and improve on the decisions already made. This is your opportunity to demonstrate that you are there to deliver by reinforcing content, operating efficiently, and increasing awareness throughout your scope in the operation areas.

> **Solutions are just as liquid as the problems they are meant to dilute...**

ROI in Action:

The operational module of an integrated listening post helps leaders understand and communicate the usage and impact of decisions that are made within each part of the organization and tie distinctly into portions of the learning module and feedback hub.

Integrated Listening Post – Operational Module

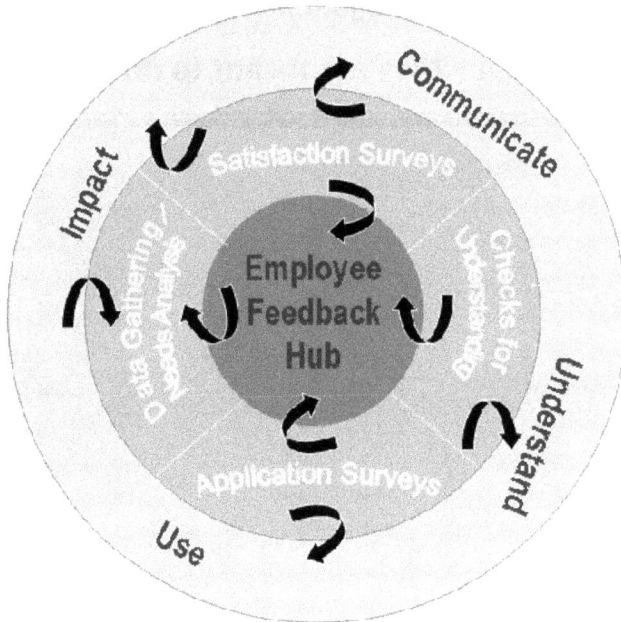

Marketing ROI

Definition: Research Methods, Open Dialogue, Integrate Messages

Key to Success: Integration

Please indicate the extent to which you agree with each of the statements below:

Question	Strongly Agree	Agree	Sometimes Agree/ Sometimes Disagree	Disagree	Strongly Disagree
Reaching projections indicates a good marketing strategy.	O	O	O	O	O
Stories are only important once the product is in the market for a period of time.	O	O	O	O	O
Branding our company is the most efficient way to increase our revenue.	O	O	O	O	O
Customer Satisfaction is the best measure of the success of a product or service.	O	O	O	O	O
Communication plans are only effective to external audiences.	O	O	O	O	O

Marketing Focus:

Being a part of the Marketing team means that you are on the forefront and backend of your company's drive for a positive return on investment. Sometimes, you are in both places at once. Your goal is to increase financial gain by advertising, sharing, and conversing with customers and clients. If you attempt this alone, you hear and experience a lack of support from your operations and training partners. Executives may wonder when will the dollars start rolling in. The key to your success is integrate, integrate, integrate.

Since your goal is to operate at maximum efficiency while growing your audience, you should not engage in marketing activities alone. In fact, you will need to talk with your partners in operations, training, and the executives prior to rolling out anything to your customers. A storyline based on the vision of the company as well as the intentions of the product or service itself will need to be created. Key message points are important for initial conversations, development of material, and building a brand. A phased timeline for your tactics is more flexible than single, disjointed resources; no matter how "pretty" they may look. Lastly, a communication plan that links each audience to your branding efforts, key messages, and story is a must. Without it, you are actually better off not doing anything at all and let word-of-mouth take effect. It is more cost-effective, but has a shorter shelf-life.

Accomplishing these tasks will require attention and cooperation. Focus on listening to the feedback from existing or potential customers to establish a storyline and key message points. This information can be found in the operations usually. Focus on understanding the difference between communication and training. If there is a change in behavior and not just a change in message, your training partners will be your best resource. Focus on understanding the direction of the company and the individual areas by working with executives on a combined strategy, creating synergy throughout your organization. This will help establish your communication timeline. By sharing the responsibility of the plan and product, you will appreciate the destination as well as the path it takes to get there...

Telling stories is better than making up a story, especially when demonstrating business results...

Chapter Four – Marketing ROI

Driving ROI:

You are headed to your favorite vacation destination in your brand-new, family car. Alas, a vacation...Unlike your drive home, work, or to the gas station, you are not alone. Your spouse, children, and various pieces of luggage have joined you in this adventure. You planned this trip all yourself and didn't tell your family where you were headed until the night before. They were so excited. No one got any sleep. You are sure that something is still plugged in at home, though it is too late to find out what...

Your driving tour has been normal. In fact, you are a little ahead of schedule and are keeping up with the transient traffic. Just then, a tiny voice from the back seat says, "I have to use the restroom..."

You look at your spouse as if to say, "Didn't we just stop?" However, the only response you receive is a shrug and, "It may be good to stretch a little too..."

Don't they know that you are almost there...well, a couple hours away, but closer than you have been...Don't they know that you have a timeline to keep, and by getting there early you could do more when you get there...Don't they know that you didn't put a credit card down to confirm the room and have to get there within the time you estimated and researched otherwise they may give away your home for the next week...Don't they know this...?

Driving ROI

All of these thoughts cease as you see a blue sign off to the right, indicating a rest area 2 miles ahead. You take the car off of cruise control and merge to the right lane. As you reach the 1 mile mark, there is another sign, slightly smaller below the rest area sign, that indicates that the next rest stop is 76 miles.

You frown, put on your directional once more and merge to the off-ramp. You guide the vehicle into a parking spot and put it in park. "Go ahead," I'll be right there," you say as your spouse and children make their way out of the vehicle.

No sooner than they are out of sight, you reach for your cell phone and try to call the resort to give them your credit card number. You select the number that you programmed into your phone and wait...and wait...and wait...

You pull the phone away from your ear and look at it...no signal. You move the phone around a little and keep looking at the signal strength. As you near the dash, two bars pop up. You press "Talk" to redial and quickly bring the phone up to your ear...within seconds, you hear beep, beep, beep indicating that you are out of range again.

Chapter Four – Marketing ROI

You lean forward and press "Talk" again. This time, you hear ringing. Within two rings, you hear, "Thank you for calling…" and the phone dies again. You shake your head in disbelief and put the phone down.

As you open the door, your spouse and children return. "I'll be right back," you say.

"Where are you going?" ask the children.

"I think that restroom break was a good idea," you mumble as you get out of the vehicle. As you near the restroom, you think to yourself, "We'll make it…"

We are so confident in a product, in a plan, sometimes we forget to share the responsibilities of its creation, planning, or success. Sometimes, we even forget to plan. However, we will certainly share the burden if it fails. We don't have a choice on this one. How often do we trust that everything will run smoothly and our family or organization will be ready to go when the product or service is ready? How often do we push the envelope on timing and forget to put down that safety net, just in case things take a little longer?

> **Businesses work like families…**
>
> **It takes a combined effort to**
>
> **Keep them strong and together…**

Driving ROI

We can research and create the most incredible marketing campaign and the most incredible product or service…sometimes in that order. However, if we don't research our partners who actually interact with the customers, the end results will be like a family without a place to stay. By waiting until the last minute to share your thoughts and plans, you run the risk of not being prepared for the trip itself. The destination or product then becomes something that is not supported and possibly resented by other parts of the team. If it is not fully supported through knowledge and understanding, your return on investment for your time and labor, let alone the time and labor of the training team, operations, and executives slowly dissipates.

In order to achieve a positive return on investment, researching methods externally is a perfect way to start planning and developing a marketing strategy with a storyline, key messages, and timeline. Opening dialogue internally will help balance resources and talent.

In the end, however, integrating messages between sources and your organization's core values will engage your customers as well as your employees. Without the engagement, all you have is a product and a plan, no positive results, and a negatively impacted ROI.

> **Strategy without values sway slightly as the breeze of change shifts with the expectations of solutions…**

Survey in Motion:

Internal buy-in and understanding are signs of a good marketing strategy…

Our employees are our customers whether we like it or not. Whether we sell things employees need or sell only to specific agencies, if the employees buy into the packaging of the product, they can ensure our customers of its quality. If they do not, the product will not sell itself for an extended period of time, if at all. We can create the best device, software package, or process. Without the support of all of our partners, we just have a product.

Projections, for the most part are short-term, short-term in the respect to the life of the company. Storylines and key messages can be reinforced at a later time while new material is created to encourage buy-in and increase positive impact. Phased timelines allow for measures to be taken at key moments of the products lifecycle. These measures are based on the key messages and branding efforts that have been developed. Measurements should not be based on arbitrary satisfaction points as this would only provide satisfaction with the company not necessarily the product or service itself.

A solid, initial storyline helps establish key message points and a brand identity…without it, they are just parts of a whole with holes… One of the best ways to open a dialogue with someone is to tell them a story. Stories that are created by one individual remain isolated to that individual until they are shared. Too often, companies believe that testimonials are the best way to market a product once it is on the market. While this helps, the company is relying on the credibility of some person in some small community who happened to share a few words, instead of the marketing team they are paying to work on a strategy. Executives can become frustrated if the product or service doesn't sell. Operators may focus their attention to other lines, other thoughts, or other concepts. Training may decide not to exhaust their training time and budget on something that doesn't have clear message points. If a story doesn't create clear message points, a behavior change will not occur. If a behavior change does not occur, your return is less than possible.

Start your story with the vision of the company or product. What does it represent? How can customers connect with the product? Research possibilities. Listen to the stories of internal and external partners to craft the meaning of the item. Key message points are just an outline or summary of your story. Both of these create and support your brand. Strong brands last because of the stories behind them.

Chapter Four – Marketing ROI

Branding a part of your organization is a piece to the long-term puzzle, not the answer to short-term finances…

Branding is the successful transition between what a product is and what you wish it to become. It is the one piece that if it sticks well, can mean a lifetime of positive press. If the branding becomes a sign of negativity, much work is needed to reinvent the product. A new look is needed. A new campaign must be established in order to distance yourself from the old brand. A new story will need to be shared, and shared, and shared, in order to create new key message points.

Integrating messages becomes more important when establishing a brand than if you are just selling a product and looking for short-term financial success. Many businesses today design posters and flyers or radio and tv ads, but do not have any other intentions other than the hope that people see the ad and experience the product. Research is conducted by independent firms to see if customers remember the company and product associated with an ad. What is being observed is that even though we can recall an ad because of an emotional connection, we may not be able to remember the product.

Reinforcement is the only way to change this behavior. So, you can either produce and distribute more ads, or you can choose multiple venues and share the key message points created from a distinct storyline and phased timeline. With the later, your brand gains momentum and is more likely to drive continued and predictable ROI rather than immediate and unstable.

Customer loyalty is the best measure of the success of a product or service...

Satisfaction only measures an immediate and isolated reaction to a product or service. Multiple measures that tie to an internal listening post build to understanding customer loyalty. These measures are developed from your storyline and key message points.

Understanding the customer experience follows satisfaction in measuring the success of a product or service. Multiple measurements over an extended period of time create your experience measures. Combine these measures with your satisfaction reports and an experience impact is realized.

Building relationships with customers through many points in time, a diverse product line, and a rich storyline is the next step of success. At this point, you will have reinforced your key messages efficiently. You will be within the last phase of your communication plan. Knowing not only what people liked, but what continues to encourage them back is important to maintaining market share and enable predictability in returns on your reinforcement investments.

Loyalty is the final measure you can establish. Once your story is shared, your internal partners have embraced your vision, and your communication efforts have been exhausted, you are ready to measure customer loyalty. By combining satisfaction results with that of experiences and relationships, you will obtain a loyalty factor and understand the breadth of your brand essence.

Communication is essential for all audiences, internal and external…
Open dialogue during the process of creating a storyline is a good way to get others in your organization involved. Share the vision and initial plot with your partners in Training and Operations as well as your Executive. You will develop a much richer story that more people want to follow and bring to life. Your key message points will drive a timeline. Your timeline will contain points at which you share your external plan with your internal partners.

Integration of messages is challenging at best if you do not engage your partners. Key messages will enable executives to understand what measurements are necessary. Communication plans shared with operators encourage ownership rather than detachment between the company and their services.

Talking is only one method of communicating…

Find out others before you finalize your

Communication Strategy…

ROI in Action:

Sharing your communication plan with your training teams will enable them to grow a learning environment and reinforce topics you wish to measure. They will help you establish an integrated internal listening post which will serve as a leading indicator of success rather than the lagging ones received from sales and customer surveys.

Integrated Listening Post – Impact Module

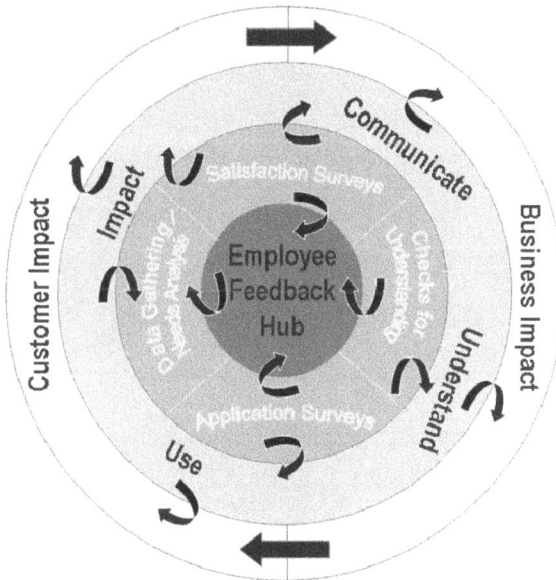

Driving Home...

Throughout this rambling, we have shared the importance of communication, listening, delivering, and integrating. While the keys to success are specified for different roles, we all need to engage in each of them if our organization is going to achieve excellence. While the specific points of ROI are important for each group, we all need to be aware of our impact on the ROI of the company.

As we go our separate ways, and this book is left on a shelf, remember the following points of summary for each team and their ROI...

A brand essence is important to a sustainable ROI. Stories are useful tools for building and maintaining a solid brand. Without stories, key messages and communication timelines become difficult tasks for the marketing team. Needs assessments that Research Methods, Open Dialogue, and Integrate Messages benefit the marketing team as they guide the organization through the meandering path of success.

Initial training results are found within satisfaction surveys and knowledge assessments. Training teams try to Recognize Impact, Organize Delivery, and Integrate Learning. Each go hand-in-hand driving our return-on-investment.

Driving Home

As the training moves more into the operations and support areas, application becomes essential. The primary functions become more aligned to Reinforcing Content, Operating Efficiently, and Increasing Awareness. Each are crucial in continuing our successes from Training and driving our organization's ROI.

When results are communicated and the executives become involved, their focus is global in nature, yet targeted at the bottom-line. The needs now center on Refining Goals, Offering Assistance, and Initiating Change. Each is intricately woven into how our organization views success and how we drive ROI.

Good luck and safe driving.

RESOURCES & TOOLS
FOR DRIVING ROI

Strategy Tool

Balanced Scorecard Structure

•   The scale (Exceeds, Meets, and Below Expectations) can be determined based on existing data with standards that are set using basic statistical methods.

•   Since the external results are greatly impacted by internal efforts, the internal evaluations possess a higher weighted impact on the final ROI.

•   Additional items can be added to the External and Business areas based on specific needs of an operation.

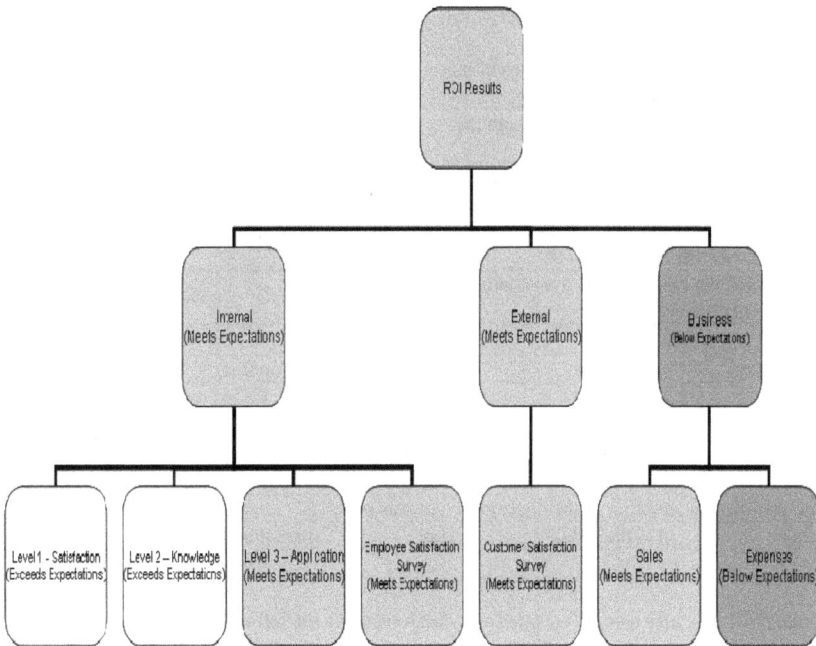

Learning Tool:

Satisfaction and Application Predictor Survey

Using the following scale, please indicate the extent to which you agree or disagree with the following statements.
SCALE: SD = Strongly Disagree, D = Disagree, DA = Sometimes Disagree/Agree, A = Agree, SA = Strongly Agree.

Content		SD	D	DA	A	SA
Q1	The material in this training connected with my learning style.	O	O	O	O	O
Q2	The flow of this learning event was easy to follow.	O	O	O	O	O
Facilitator(s)		SD	D	DA	A	SA
Q3	The facilitators presented information clearly.	O	O	O	O	O
Q4	The facilitators were organized.	O	O	O	O	O
Q5	The facilitator engaged me during this learning event.	O	O	O	O	O
Overall		SD	D	DA	A	SA
Q7	This learning event was a good use of my time.	O	O	O	O	O
Q8	I understand how this learning event has prepared me to perform my role.	O	O	O	O	O
Q9	I participated as much as possible in this learning event.	O	O	O	O	O
Q10	I feel prepared to use the information I learned in this learning event.	O	O	O	O	O
Q11	I feel empowered applying the information I learned in this learning event.	O	O	O	O	O
Q12	Considering everything, I am satisfied with this learning event.	O	O	O	O	O

The Pace of this learning event:				
Much too slow	Too slow	Just Right	Too fast	Much too fast
O	O	O	O	O

The Length of this learning event:				
Much too short	Too short	Just Right	Too long	Much too long
O	O	O	O	O

How much of the information in this learning event was new:				
None	Less than Half	Half	More than half	All
O	O	O	O	O

On a scale of 1 to 10, how would you rate your skill level using the information learned in this event? (1=low, 10= high)

On a scale of 1 to 10, how certain are you about the estimate in the preceding question? (1=low, 10= high)

Resources & Tools for Driving ROI

Satisfaction and Application Predictor Survey continued...

Using the following scale, please indicate the extent to which you agree or disagree with the following statements.
SCALE: SD = Strongly Disagree, D = Disagree, DA = Sometimes Disagree/Agree, A = Agree, SA = Strongly Agree.

This training has enabled me to apply the following:	SD	D	DA	A	SA
Statement for Learning Objective 1.	O	O	O	O	O
Statement for Learning Objective 2.	O	O	O	O	O
Statement for Learning Objective 3.	O	O	O	O	O
Statement for Learning Objective 4.	O	O	O	O	O
Statement for Learning Objective 5.	O	O	O	O	O

Please share one to two pieces of this learning event that were MOST important to you.

Please share one to two pieces of this learning event that were LEAST important to you.

Please share any comments about the content, facilitator(s), or overall learning event below.

Operational Tool

Competency-Focused Learning Plan

Front-line Employee – Focus on Customer Satisfaction

Observations	Impacts to role	Competencies
•	•	•
•	•	•
•	•	•
Resources to impact and understand role:		
•		
•		

Front-line Supervisor – Focus on customer experience

Observations	Impacts to role	Competencies
•	•	•
•	•	•
•	•	•
Resources to impact and understand role:		
•		
•		

Manager – Focus on customer relationship

Observations	Impacts to role	Competencies
•	•	•
•	•	•
•	•	•
Resources to impact and understand role:		
•		
•		

Resources & Tools for Driving ROI

Impact Tool

Communication Plan – Line Item

Storyline Link/Business Objective:

Resource:

Key Message:

Date Shared:

Anticipated Delivery Date:

Key Partners:

Expected Results:

Actual Results:

Gap Analysis:

www.ingramcontent.com/pod-product-compliance
Lightning Source LLC
Chambersburg PA
CBHW060644210326
41520CB00010B/1728

To protect my valued clients, managers, and salespersons and honor their privacy, I've changed the names of those persons that appear throughout the book.

Published by Rick Charnack

ISBN: 978-0-6159132-2-3

Cover design by Rick Charnack
Typeset by Gary A. Rosenberg • www.thebookcouple.com

RICKRADIO CONFIDENTIAL

Confessions of an Ad Man

Rick Charnack

CONTENTS

Part 2—The "High" Eighties

For my daughter, Liza

AUTHOR'S NOTE

Stepping back from a career in radio sales and sales management that spanned over three decades, I thought it might be amusing to take a look at some of the unique characters and zany experiences I encountered during my career. And, what follows, are seventeen years' worth of stories that run the gamut of my humble beginnings to a sales manager.

What first came to mind was the very beginning of my career at a station in Providence, Rhode Island, where my sales manager knew less about radio sales than I did. Needless to say, I wasn't enthralled about the business and spent most of my time thinking about alternate career choices. It wasn't until I joined one of America's top radio companies at their Fort Lauderdale, Florida, station where my education about radio sales accelerated and results thereby followed. Once I learned the business and began helping others with conceptual ideas that garnered sales, I chose to accept a position as sales manager at WINZ AM and FM (I-95FM) in Miami.

The unique stories that follow are an honest look back at experiences I had dealing with sometimes outlandish clients, station management, and salespersons. Many were fueled with social "lubricants" such as alcohol and drugs. At the time, it was a way of life and success. Little did I know that they would ultimately take their toll.

My hope is that you'll enjoy the variety of situations I've included in this book, no matter what your career focus might be (or has taken you). If you've worked in broadcast sales, great! Or if you are new to broadcast sales, I hope you'll find my candid tales and observations as humorous as I did looking back at them.

INTRODUCTION

She ran around the office shouting, "I've sold a package! I've sold a package!" Such was the typical outpouring of emotion attached to the sale of the intangible product: radio advertising.

What drives a person to become skilled in the sale of advertising, especially since it is evolved simply from air? Perhaps it's an unquenchable thirst for helping a customer's business grow. Or is it the pride of representing a respected radio station in a town where personalities are exciting and popular? For me, it was neither. At the time I plunged into radio sales, it was only an attraction to the steady income following my former college career as a "C" student.

My reasons for entering the business end of radio were somewhat of a contradiction. Having earned a bachelor's degree from a business college without much interest in business, I turned to my love of music and favorite pastime: music radio. While growing up in New Jersey, I'd tune my clock radio to stations from far-off places, including Buffalo, Dallas, and Detroit. I loved listening to personalities like The Weird Beard, Jackson Armstrong, Dan Ingram, Scott Muni, and Cousin Brucie. Listening to New York's 77 WABC had kindled the dream that someday I'd follow in their footsteps behind a microphone.

While at college, I deejayed at Brown University's college station and, following graduation, worked a short stint at a hometown station in New Jersey. On-air announcing was my first love, but in the end it was an invitation to return to Providence, Rhode Island, the same city where I had attended college, to investigate a radio "account executive" position that would eventually commence my career in radio-advertising sales.

Since I was anything but goal directed, I began investigating my opportunity with trepidation and soon discovered that the title *account executive* was actually a lofty synonym for *salesperson*. The idea of living life as an account executive at the station had made a big impression on a friend who had been a news announcer at the same college station where I worked. He was apparently acting on my behalf when he arranged for my introduction to the station sales manager.

The Providence station sales manager and I spoke in generalities on the phone, and he invited me to Rhode Island to interview for the job. He rolled out the red carpet when I arrived, and that evening I sat in first-row seats to watch the Providence College Friars play an exciting basketball game. It was almost as if he were selling me to come to work for him. *Wasn't this supposed to be the other way around?*

At times I wondered what it was about this account executive position that I believed could change my life? More importantly, how could I exchange my comfortable, patched denim jeans for the conservative attire befitting an account executive?

I was appreciative of the introduction from my college friend, although quite uneasy about what was ahead. How could I leave behind my love of announcing for a career in sales, something I knew nothing about—and feared the most?

Part 1

THE SEVENTIES

Chapter 1

MY FIRST MANAGER

Following my hiring (the $200-weekly salary filled me with a sense of abundance), I embarked on my new career track. And, although I had committed to life as a radio salesperson, I continued to fantasize about life as a deejay.

It didn't help that my first sales manager, Carl Greenbaum, was a complete buffoon. You know the type: a vain character hired to front the sales department and make a good impression on customers. Ironically, in his case, it was a toupee adorning his head that advertisers viewed as a turnoff, unless one was confidence inspired by viewing a ludicrous rug job.

"Why don't you come into my office so that we can talk?" suggested Carl several days following my arrival. (Until then our discussions were confined to completing forms for the corporation.)

"Sure, Carl," I replied, after standing and pulling on a wedgie that my new wool slacks had manifested while sitting at my desk.

In his office, I noticed how spotless and orderly articles were lined up on his desk and shelves. I then observed his nervous habit of picking stray lint from his socks. It was rumored that he had acquired the talent of "lint swatting" during his former career as a weekend weatherman on a local television station. As part of his weatherman makeup routine,

4

Carl would pick off lint as if he had a nervous tick, never denying his viewers a picture of his well-dressed, lint-free perfection.

"So what do you think so far?" Carl inquired.

"So far everything's terrific." *Actually it's all great except I've now uncovered your obsession for removing lint from your clothes.* "It will be even better when I can find my way around the offices."

The station was located on the top floor of an eight-story building where floors one through seven were dedicated to retail sales for which the company was famous. At one time the floor had housed the accounting and administrative offices, but they had been renovated when the company purchased the radio station and a television station. As a result of age and poorly designed space, the radio sales offices were located through a series of narrow hallways and matchbox-size offices that were accessed only by navigating small steps.

Since this was the first one-on-one meeting with Carl, I had dutifully arrived in his office with a notebook, ready to soak in some of his sales wisdom.

"Rick, you know I brought you back to Providence because my gut tells me that you are one of the winners," he offered, picking stray lint off one of his socks.

"Thanks, Carl. And I think I've joined a winning team here." *P L E A S E!—Stop picking lint off your clothes!*

"I've got big plans for you, Rick. Just observe the team for the first ninety days or so. I'm certain you'll get the hang of it."

"Sure, Carl. Do you suggest I follow anyone in particular?" As the words left my mouth, I was interrupted by Carl's ringing telephone. He picked up the receiver, motioned for me to leave his office, and leaned back in his chair, eyes on his lint-free slacks.

There were other occasions when Carl and I would conference in his office. His lint-swat move would always annoy me.
It only served to reinforce the discomfort I was feeling from
my transformation to an "account executive." Sitting in his
office, wearing more clothing at one time than I had during
my entire four years of college—undershirt, boxer shorts, over-
the-calf socks, button-down collared pinpoint oxford dress
shirt, wool slacks with cuffs, imitation alligator belt, diagonally
striped tie, wing-tip shoes, and suit jacket. I couldn't remember a time when I felt so uncomfortable and out of place.

One cold and gray rainy afternoon—a constant during the
winter months in Rhode Island—Carl summoned me into his
office at lunchtime.

"Have you been to the Knife and Fork yet?" he asked.

"No," I answered. "Isn't that the place where many station
staffers have lunch?"

"Yes, it is. And I'd like to take you there to 'bust your
cherry.' " *Great! Now he's a comedian. . . .*

"Sure," I responded, "let me get my overcoat."

After I retrieved my overcoat from the sales office, Carl
and I walked to the elevator and took it to the ground floor,
exiting through an apparent crowd of shoppers waiting for the
rain to stop. Reluctantly, Mr. Weatherman/Sales Manager and
I crossed a slush-filled downtown Providence Street. I recall
his expression upon seeing a feather on his overcoat. Because
he might see one of his adoring weekend weatherman fans,
Carl would never stand for such a hindrance to his sartorial
splendor. In a gazelle-like move, with ease he swiped off the
feather of duck, goose, or whatever animal had been deprived
of it. *What a vain character!*

"Here we are," Carl offered as we checked our coats, "the
famous Knife and Fork."

We walked over to the hostess, and I watched him plant

a big kiss on her cheek. She smiled but quickly pulled away as if Carl had bad breath. *Perhaps you should pay as much attention to your breath as your socks.*

"Your usual booth, Mr. Greenbaum?" she inquired.

"Yes!" Carl said with a giggle. "But, as I've always told you, please call me Carl."

We followed the hostess, who sat us at his "usual booth" in the middle of the restaurant where he could see and be seen by all who were having lunch. A waitress quickly walked over.

"Rick, have a Bloody Mary," he suggested. "They are fantastic here!"

"No, thanks. I'll have an iced tea," I responded.

"Bring on my favorite," confirmed Carl, "and a backup as well."

Following a couple of hours watching him ingest multiple Bloody Mary cocktails and flank steak, he began functioning in less than full-motor capacity. In fact, the severity with which he was slurring his words even startled the waitress. Until that moment, she and Carl had been ever so indiscreetly flirting with their eyes and "love you" looks. How inspiring— my imbibed mentor in his rug-adorned head panting after someone I guessed to be a Providence beauty-school dropout.

After finishing lunch and paying the check, Carl needed assistance standing, so I reached over and steadied him. As he stumbled to the coatroom, I gazed at his eyes and saw they were of the watery and bloodshot variety.

"I've got this one," I said and handed our coat-check tag to a waiting older woman. "Here's your coat, Carl."

As we exited the restaurant, I noticed a large piece of fur on my overcoat, probably surrendered from another coat while hanging in the coatroom. Recognizing Carl's now compromised visual capabilities, I decided to help him play victim to his own silly vanity. Seizing the opportunity, I quickly removed it and attached it to the back of his overcoat with a quick move that would impress a member of Cirque du Soleil. How could he wear a less-than-perfect overcoat? Would it cause his demise as he walked along the sidewalks of Providence, nodding at others as a weatherman might do with his audience?

Approaching our office building, five or six station employees were returning from lunch and gathering at the entrance to the station building. As we all entered the elevator, I overheard the giggles of several staff members who were staring at the newly furred adornment on Carl's coat.

"What happened to your overcoat?" asked a staff member.

"Guess the cat died," suggested another.

"What do you mean?" protested Carl. *He doesn't have a clue!*

As we walked back into the station offices, Carl's secretary, Marilyn, spotted the feather on his overcoat.

"Got that lint roller handy," she said. "I need to roll off a large piece of fur."

"Oh, I see," Carl grumbled. "I was wondering why people were laughing in the elevator. How embarrassing!"

You were wondering? After only a few days on the job *I* was wondering what I was doing working for Carl and why I had made a decision to take the "account executive" job in Rhode Island. What I really needed was a manager who could "show me the sales ropes," not someone who was more interested in his vanity.

I then asked myself, *What the hell am I doing here? And how could I have so quickly "sold out" to a job where dining with a manager might include such drama?*

Chapter 2

THE FIRST SALES CALL

I suppose I had more faith in Carl Greenbaum, the ex-weekend weatherman turned sales manager, than I'm letting on. After all, he had given me my first break in the business. Besides, it was on his recommendation that the company paid for me to attend the Radio Advertising Bureau's "School for Radio Account Executives." The weeklong course took place on the campus of New Jersey's Rutgers University and included selling tips from purported sales gurus from the Radio Advertising Bureau, the industry's sales resource. The New Brunswick campus was beautiful, but the instructors ran a close second to Carl's ineptness.

During the seminar, most of the presenters showed up dressed in flashy suits and even some with slicked hair. I started to believe that the radio industry promoted executives based on looks and not talent. *Perfect . . . I'm being instructed on how to emulate Carl!*

However, I wondered how I might nattily dress to project the look of radio sales professional, and came away from the training with only a small amount of new sales skills but some great ideas on how to mix and match wardrobe colors.

Shortly after returning from Rutgers, I was taught an important lesson in salesmanship. I had picked up the basics in college and at Rutgers, but the idea of calling on Rhode Island's old timers—still fond of Brylcream—seemed a daunting task. However, my instincts for survival toppled my fear of failure as I was soon in my suit prepared to test my "freshly minted" radio-selling skills in Providence.

Upon arrival back at the station following my training, I eagerly awaited a meeting with Carl to discuss what I had learned. I waited outside his office until he signaled me to come in. Sitting in one of his office chairs, I noticed he was removing lint with a rolling device. With legs crossed on his desk, he pressed it to a sock to remove a patch of lint that had gathered just below his hair-covered leg.

"How did you enjoy the week of training?" he inquired.

"It was terrific!" I responded, with my fingers crossed behind my back to protect me from the lie.

"What part did you find especially helpful?"

I barely got a word in before his phone rang. He picked up the receiver and started to jabber. I patiently waited to speak with him. After observing his phony smile and demonstrative hands for ten minutes, I stood up and bolted for my desk. Reasoning that I had better things to do than listen to his discourse on the phone and be subjected to his body hair, I left.

With the belief that my training had prepared me for the next step—going out to see clients face-to-face—I packed up my sales kit and exited the office. Without a briefing and information session (Carl was still on the phone), I ventured out to make a sales call at an automobile dealership in Cranston. The dealership was on a list of prospective accounts that Carl had assured me offered a potentially large opportunity. The account, Esposito Oldsmobile, was known for its slogan "Tony E: The Man with Your New Car Key!"

Following a thirty-minute drive to the dealership, I entered the showroom, dressed to kill, and ready to dazzle this unsuspecting prospective customer and approached the receptionist.

"I'd like to speak with the advertising decision maker," I proposed, just as I had learned at Rutgers.

"That would be the general manager," she responded. "Do you have an appointment?"

"No, but I'll be happy to wait to see him," I replied.

"You can wait over there by the sales offices," she said, pointing to an area of the showroom where six chairs were lined up against a dealership window. I noticed my old Volvo parked outside, a striking contrast to the array of brand-new Oldsmobiles parked in close proximity.

At Rutgers, I had heard stories of businesses fending off salespersons by having them wait for an insufferable amount of time. Sellers would eventually become impatient and leave. Not me! I was determined to see the general manager no matter how long it took.

After thirty minutes of waiting, I was greeted not by the manager, but a salesperson. What I didn't realize was that the general manager was famous for pushing his salespeople on unsuspecting solicitors, hoping to sell them a car.

"Can I help you?" he asked.

"Yes," I responded. "I'm here to speak with the advertising decision maker."

"Oh, right, he'll be with you in a few minutes," he responded with a chuckle.

The salesman, based on his outdated sport coat and poorly ironed shirt, both of which reinforced my idea of why I never aspired to join the profession, proceeded to test my tolerance by literally dragging me over to a new model on the showroom floor.

"Why don't you sit in this brand-new Cutlass?" he suggested. "You'll never drive a Volvo again."

How did this guy know that I drove a Volvo? He must have been on the lookout! In fact, during the forty-five-minute period that followed, he was somehow able to hoist me into each new car in the showroom.

Just as I was about to expire from his breath—the result of an obviously onion-laden sandwich—and the sight of his cigarette-stained teeth, I dashed over to grab my briefcase and overcoat and headed for the door. No general manager, no meeting, and no presentation. *Oh, no, I just screwed up my first sales call!*

Back in my six-year-old Volvo, I sped away defeated and feeling sorry for myself. My self-pity wasn't based solely on rejection but on an early career realization that I couldn't afford a brand-new Oldsmobile Cutlass.

Due to my stubbornness (more like my will to survive), I returned to Esposito Oldsmobile the following week. This time, nothing was going to stop me, and I had come with a clear mission: to sell commercials on my radio station!

Once again, I was escorted to the waiting area to sit for a half-hour, after which time the same auto salesman walked over to me.

"This could be your lucky day," he announced. "We're offering great prices on all new Cutlasses today only. Let me show you this black-on-black over here in the showroom."

"Now wait!" I protested. "You're not going to try this maneuver on me again! I've already been held hostage by your tactics and would prefer not to have you escort me around the showroom again!"

After I further revealed the details of my past week's experience, he quickly maneuvered away from the car and began to buddy-up to me with a rambling version of his career in car sales. I actually had pity on the man when he told me about his recent hemorrhoid surgery, which he described as the "Roto-Rooter."

At the tender age of twenty-three, my only experience with hemorrhoids had been Preparation H television ads. How could I possibly relate to his backside problem? Did he acquire his condition through frequent test drives? No doubt I showed my naïveté at that early age.

I wasn't able to sell a radio schedule at the dealership or even meet with the general manager. However, to this day, whenever I see a Roto-Rooter television ad, I think of "Tony E: The Man with Your New Car Key!" and my brief experience with an Oldsmobile salesman who had a hemorrhoid problem. I still wonder why I believed that a hemorrhoid removal procedure was related to a twirling wire that cleared a clogged drain.

But, most of all, I think about that black-on-black Cutlass and how my life might have magically changed had I been able to afford it.

Chapter 3

WEEKEND IN MIAMI

Around October 1, when the leaves began to fall off the Rhode Island trees and a gray pallor fell over the landscape, I began longing for a warmer, more hospitable climate. Realizing that a weekend fix might be all that was necessary, I contacted my friend Ron in Miami.

Ron was someone who could always provide me with some laughs and participation in his decadent lifestyle. Since the station would be closed on Monday because of Columbus Day, I decided it would be best to celebrate a holiday weekend of my own in Miami. I couldn't understand why Rhode Island took this holiday so seriously. Gas stations, convenience stores, retail stores, and supermarkets were closed on Columbus Day. If you were searching for coffee and a bear claw anywhere in the state, you'd be mightily disappointed.

Trying to be discreet, I waited until there were no staff members at the elevator and took it to the ground floor. The station building fronted Weybosset Street, a main street in Providence, and directly across the street were stores and offices that included a travel agency. I entered the travel agency and was greeted by an agent wearing a plaid skirt and turtleneck sweater. Her outfit was far afield from the sexy clothing I looked forward to seeing in Miami.

"I'd like to book a flight to Miami for Friday night," I told the agent.

"That shouldn't be a problem," she replied. "There's a flight that leaves Providence at 8 p.m. and arrives in Miami at 10:30 p.m. Will that work for you?" she asked.

"It certainly will," I eagerly agreed.

Following a quick telephone call (I presumed to the airline), she took a blank ticket from her desk drawer and proceeded to complete it. I paid with my credit card.

"One round-trip ticket to Miami," she said loud enough for everyone at the agency to hear. I stood, left the agency, and walked back to the station.

Once again, my naïveté got the best of me. It turned out that Carl often visited the same agency. In fact, it didn't take long for the word to get back to him that his rookie had planned a trip to Florida. *Oh no, I'm busted. . . . He knows I'm about ready to go away—perhaps for good!*

As I walked through the sales department hallway, he was standing next to my secretary with a wry look on his face. He had apparently received a call from the travel agency and was waiting for me outside his office.

"I bet you didn't know it, Rick, but my grandparents have a condo in Fort Lauderdale. Since you're going to be in the neighborhood this weekend, could you call and say hello for me?"

He burst out laughing. Then his secretary, Marilyn, laughed. Then Wendy, who had arrived from the copy and production department, laughed.

So what if they knew I was traveling to Florida? How could I resist leaving the barren landscape and impossible job situation for a warmer climate riddled with visual treats?

What they didn't know was that I had made a decision to

canvass Miami's radio market and take my multi-months' sales experience to a completely new locale. On Columbus Day, most businesses, including radio stations in Miami, were open for business, and I imagined my chances of locating a radio manager who would be willing to meet with me were good. I had already copied several pages of the SRDS, radio's white pages of stations listed by city. Included were the names of sales managers, so I could easily identify whom I wanted to call.

I decided to impress Ron to show off my "look of success" by wearing one of my new wool suits. As soon as I packed my bag, I was off to the airport. The two-and-a-half-hour flight from Providence to Miami was uneventful, and after we landed and stopped at the gate, I stood and pulled down my alpaca overcoat from the overhead bin. As soon as the jet door was opened, the evening's humidity dashed any hope of impressing Ron; my shirt was now glued to my back.

Walking into the gate area, I immediately recognized Ron. He was the one in the Hawaiian shirt standing next to a scantily dressed blonde. She was hanging all over him like a puppy dog in heat.

"Hi, Ron," I said. "It's great to see you." *Can you see me? Is there anything behind those sunglasses that resemble eyes?*

"Oh, hi, Rick," he murmured. "Wonderful to see you. Let's get your suitcase. By the way, this is Jill. Say hi to Rick, Jill."

"Hi, Rick," offered Jill with an obvious slur.

After I claimed my luggage, sweat was pouring from seemingly every part of my body as I carried my suitcase into the parking garage. Ron assured me that we were taking a shortcut to his new car. Following a recent divorce, Ron had yet to "find himself" and was cavorting with any blonde who would smile at him. We walked by several rows of cars, and he pointed out his. There it was: a very yellow, very used, Vega.

A used Vega? I chuckled when thinking of the roaring laughter from the salesman's office as Ron drove away from the dealership, blue smoke pouring from the tailpipe. Hoisting my suitcase into the backseat (the hatchback lock wasn't working), I climbed in for the ride back to his apartment.

The blonde—er, Jill—began to shout out half-sentences between puffs of her menthol Kool cigarettes. I had always wondered if smoking Kools helped one radiate coolness. I speculated that if someone saw you and your pack of Kools, the person would smile and nod, as if a secret language existed between the two of you. I'm not knocking Kools. One evening I had opted for some coolness, smoked half a pack, and vomited all night. I also contracted a case of bronchitis that lasted a month. I never conjured up the nerve to take even a drag from a Kool cigarette again. In the car, however, the blonde seemed very cool, wafting clouds of cigarette smoke my way.

The Vega's air conditioning was losing its battle with the evening's humidity, and sweat had now fully saturated most of my body. I cursed myself for the decision to wear a wool suit and desperately wanted to shed some clothing. Had it not been for the lightheadedness I was feeling from cigarette smoke and the Vega's exhaust, I might have had the strength to do so.

Exiting the highway and passing through a residential neighborhood, Ron mumbled something. I asked him to repeat what he had said.

"My place is just ahead," he said again. Ron turned into his rental community. "We're here!" he shouted, turning into a parking space. I heard the Vega's power steering let out a groan. *Thank G-d we're here!*

"Let's get out of this heat," I said, perspiration dripping from my body.

I wondered what type of accommodations were in store for

me and had already resigned myself to sleeping on Ron's sofa for the next several days. I didn't know, however, that his roommate Alan often spent evenings on the sofa with women he'd picked up only hours earlier at trendy Miami clubs. I had to hand it to him. As a good-looking guy whose problem with alcohol impinged his ability to put two sentences together, Alan managed to charm and seduce many a Miami beauty. Ron warned me that I might somehow be preempted from my space on the sofa because Alan would often wind up passing out from the effects of his usual "cocktail" before a second kiss. This unloving act of indifference would send many beauties out the door as he lay passed out on the sofa.

By the time we parked, it was almost midnight. Following a quick elevator ride to the third floor, we turned right and stopped at the fifth apartment door.

"Hello," said Ron as we entered the apartment. No answer.

"Alan?" Rob shouted.

No response.

Walking into the living room, we discovered Alan sleeping on what was to be my bed. Ron tried to wake him . . . still no response.

"Take his feet," Ron said. "I'll pick him up by his shoulders."

Ron and I clumsily moved Alan into his bedroom and onto the bed. *So this is what it feels like to move a dead body!*

I watched Ron walk to Alan's closet, gather a blanket and pillow, and throw them on the sofa.

"Goodnight, Rick!" he cried out. "Welcome to Miami. We've got some wild plans for tomorrow night. I think you'll enjoy them. Get some sleep because you're going to need it!" With that said, he walked to the bedroom and closed the door. *Guess the blonde awaits!*

Chapter 4

HOLD THE CHAMPAGNE!

I was awakened on Saturday morning by loud voices coming from the kitchen. Apparently Ron and Alan were discussing evening plans.

"We might go to The Planet for dinner and dance at Passion," Alan suggested.

"That might be too much. How about we do dinner at The Planet and go from there," replied Ron.

After a few minutes of additional discussion, they settled on meeting some friends for dinner at The Planet, one of Miami's trendy clubs, where I'd be introduced to several of Miami's beautiful and eligible girls.

"Here's the plan," contributed Alan. "We'll do breakfast, poolside and backgammon until four, shower, dress, and have dinner at nine p.m."

"Deal," confirmed Ron.

Standing up from the sofa bed, I nodded Ron my approval of the plan. The thought of spending an evening with beautiful Miami women started to ease the tension I'd brought from Providence.

We spent the afternoon lying in the sun, "catching rays" being the well-known vernacular. After several hours of doing so, I was feeling the effects of those rays. Combined with the pasty skin I brought along from my tenure in Rhode Island, it was obvious that I needed to take shelter under an umbrella by the pool.

I spent the remainder of the day reading and, between chapters, observing Alan's unsuccessful cavorting with female residents of the apartment complex who were more interested in tanning. *This guy never stops!*

That evening we arrived at The Planet and assembled at a table adjacent to the dance floor. It was set back from the dance floor with just enough room for club patrons to cruise by within view without disturbing us. Two unattached girls who knew Alan joined us as we were seated. There were eight of us: Ron, Jill, Alan with two hot college girls (they looked very young and were wearing gold necklaces, each with a "UM"—University of Miami—pendant), two unattached girls, and myself. I started to talk with one of the girls whose name was Carolina (she pronounced her name Car-o-leena) who, as it turned out wasn't from Florida, spoke with a Spanish accent, and was probably Cuban. She and her friend, Maria, were both wearing sunglasses that hindered my seeing and conversing with either of them. I reasoned they might be wearing them to look "Hollywood" or hide their reddened eyes.

Alan made a short announcement welcoming his new friend from Rhode Island (that was me) and opened what appeared to be an expensive bottle of champagne. Having had a glass or two of champagne during my drinking career, I was usually careful to drink it only after I had consumed food. Alan's suggestion to drink before the meal was for "maximum effect." I questioned his judgment but followed along. He opened the bottle and, with a huge "pop," sent bubbles into Ron's girlfriend's glass.

The champagne ingestion strategy soon paid off. He ordered several more bottles, and everyone was loosening up.

Carolina and Maria were laughing hysterically and attracting men, many wearing garish gold chains that included Stars of David and oversized pinky rings. It was a sight that made me almost deny my own Jewish roots. Jill was blowing smoke rings in Ron's face between long and lurid kisses, and Alan's dates were becoming very chummy with each other. I did my part by holding a roll in front of Carolina.

"Have a bite," I said, suggesting that she taste a roll. She took a slow, suggestive bite, and it wasn't long before I was helping both Carolina and Maria take long, erotic bites.

By the time the food had arrived, none of us remembered what had been ordered. The place was getting very noisy as other dinner and club customers arrived. The crowd looked very Miami—men wore shirts with buttons open to show off their chest and gold chains. Women wore short skirts and high platform shoes. *What a scene!* The music level had been turned up. People were bunched around, and the dance floor was beginning to fill up. Music seemed to be blasting from everywhere. The deejay had changed his selections from soft jazz to loud disco. "For the Love of Money" had the dance floor filling up. . . . *For the love of money, people will steal from their mother, for the love of money, people will rob their own brother!*

Thinking it might be a good idea to put some food in my body, I looked at my dinner plate and picked up my silverware.

"Whoops," I said, as a knife slid out of my grip to the floor. Scouring the table for a replacement utensil, I spied a butter knife. I picked it up, tried to cut my steak, and failed miserably.

"We're going over to dance!" Carolina and Maria cried out as they vanished into the crowd with two muscle-bodies, whose opened shirts revealed sparse black hairs.

Alan was leaning back, his eyes rolling into his head. Ron was laughing uncontrollably.

"Try one of these," he said, dispensing a large white pill to each of the girls.

"I'll take one," I requested. Alan handed me a pill that I swallowed with a slug of champagne. *Let's get this party started!* Soon everyone at our table gave up on dinner and headed to the dance floor, and in no time we were all cavorting to "Dancing Machine." It probably wasn't a pretty sight, but the freedom that flailing arms and shuffling feet brought us made it all worthwhile.

To revisit my travails for the remainder of the evening would be much too painful. Suffice it to say that the club layout included a very long stairway to an upstairs bar. After climbing the stairs, I soon regretted leaving the safer confines of our table and, while standing, realized in terror that, at some point, it would be necessary to walk down the stairs. *Oh, hell, I'll have another drink and worry about it later.*

Soon I had ingested more alcohol than I thought possible, and my condition had me wrecked.

"Anyone care for a drink?" I blurted out. "How come my 'twin' friends aren't here?" I inquired.

As I stumbled around the upstairs bar, I recognized no one, sought out anyone who would drink with me, and began bastardizing my family name. At some point I crushed any remaining self-esteem by suggesting that any one of the single women at the bar carry my baby. The comment was met with disgust on many of their faces. *Guess that wasn't a good idea. I wonder whether it might work for Alan.* Only one, not the prettiest of the bunch, smiled back at me. I smiled back but quickly paid the tab and made my move to the stairs to return to the table.

In a gallant attempt to descend the long stairway, I lost

my footing and went tumbling down. *Wow . . . this is embarrassing!* My crumpled body had attracted several customers to the foot of the stairs. I apparently hadn't suffered any injuries or the alcohol had blurred my senses. (Probably the latter.) Surprisingly, the fall didn't startle many patrons, as it happened frequently at the club. Ron had somehow heard the commotion and made his way through the thick club crowd to check it out.

"Stand up," he said, as he bent over to help me.

I grabbed his hand, and my weight caused him to lose his balance and fall to the floor beside me.

Several large men wearing black suits were now hovering over us. Each extended one of their monster-size hands and swooped Ron and me back on our feet. We were escorted to the front door of the club and out into the Miami night. I shouted out, "Hey 'weekend weatherman,' wherever you are, this is how we party in Miami!"

Chapter 5

MIAMI INTERVIEW

Following our drunk-fest on Saturday night, I spent most of Sunday on the sofa, recovering and watching the Miami Dolphins get trounced by the New York Jets. Alan joined me on the sofa and offered me a Quaalude.

"This will fix you right up," he said. "It's a proven hangover fixer." *Surely I can't trust this guy. He spent last night barely conscious. But then again, so did I!*

Knowing that I needed to be at my best the following day, I declined his offer. It was tough turning down a Quaalude, but shortly after swallowing several pills, I observed him lose all sense of motion for the entire afternoon. He finally went into his bedroom, closed the door, and emerged late in the afternoon just in time for dinner. Ron had ordered Chinese food that we all quickly devoured. We opted for staying at home that night.

On Monday morning, I grabbed a cup of coffee at the apartment and the *Miami Herald* that Ron had left on the kitchen table. While rummaging through the classified ads, I noticed a number of phone sales jobs that promised $50,000 income in the first year. *No phone room jobs for me. I want to see customers face to face!*

Following Rob and Alan's departure for work, I turned to the yellow pages to research radio station telephone numbers.

My strategy was to set a minimum of three face-to-face meetings before the day was over. My telephone contact with a sales manager would go like this:

"I'm in Miami today visiting with stations and would like to meet with you to discuss a sales position." If I heard just a bit of hesitation, I would add, "Do you have a member of your sales staff that's just not measuring up? Let's meet today while I'm in town to discuss how I might upgrade your team!" By 9:30, I had set two appointments, one for 11:00 a.m. and one for 2:00 p.m.

Rob had agreed to let me use his car for the day as long as I filled the tank with gas. Upon starting the car, I noticed the gas gauge needle was below the "E," dictating a quick stop at the closest gas station. *Arrghhh. I could have taken care of this yesterday!* There was a station a few blocks from Rob's apartment, and I pulled in. While filling the Vega's tank, I realized that perspiration was already gathering on the back of my shirt. Although I had packed a lightweight suit, I was convinced that the humidity was out to get me. *Just stay cool, Rick.* After gassing up, I headed toward my first appointment at WBSG.

Bill Trent, WBSG's local sales manager, had described their offices as an old brick building on Brickell Avenue, in downtown Miami, the same street lined with stunning, contemporary, glass structures.

It didn't take long for me to find the station. I could see why Bill had made a point of describing the contrast between buildings. The station's offices were clearly out of character for the neighborhood and resembled something out of a suburban town in New England.

I parked Ron's car in a visitor's spot and walked around to the front entrance. When I opened the door into the reception area, I detected a musty smell that I later learned was common in older buildings in Miami. None could survive the acrid heat and humidity. The building lobby featured walls of dark wood paneling. Toward the back was a five-foot-tall wraparound receptionist's desk. A flashing neon WBSG sign was affixed to one of the walls. Music from the station was playing through a small speaker behind the receptionist.

I noticed a young woman's head behind a desk so high I could lean on it. Further advance revealed caked makeup adorning her cheeks. She held the phone receiver to her ear and was laughing and speaking in Spanish. *"Usted debe ver lo que él me compró."* (You should see what he bought me), she said. *"Una pulsera muy barata!"* (A very cheap bracelet.) Noticing me, she spoke into the phone and said, "Gotta go," in perfect English. *Oh, I see. You DO have the ability to speak to gringos in their native tongue!*

"May I help you?" she asked.

"Yes," I said. "I have an appointment with Bill Trent."

She dialed a number on a large receptionist phone, and I overheard her page traveling throughout the lobby and an open door directly in back of her. "Bill Trent, you have a guest in the lobby." She hung up and suggested that I have a seat on one of the chairs.

I walked over and sat on a chair upholstered with faded paisley fabric. The wood paneling directly behind the chair showed wear marks where the chair had rubbed up against it. Gazing around, I noticed all of the lobby area chairs had created a similar effect on the paneled wall directly in back of them.

It wasn't long before the elevator doors opened to reveal a tall, middle-aged man with slumped shoulders, open-collar shirt, and short hair, not unlike that of an armed forces cut. The elevator doors closed as he walked into the room, glancing toward me.

"Rick, I'm Bill Trent. Let's go upstairs. We'll be meeting with Harvey Greene, he's the general sales manager."

"Great," I said, following him onto the elevator, and watched him press an elevator button with a very worn "2."

"Guess you found the place okay," he said. "I told you we had a very distinctive look for the street."

"Yes, you do!" *And I'm certain it won't be long until it's earmarked for demolition. What a dump!*

We exited the elevator into a suite of small offices with two desks in each and proceeded down a hallway leading to a corner office. Bill stopped and allowed me to enter first. Standing behind the desk was a man with handsome facial features, slicked gray hair, and an iridescent suit, clearly reminiscent of the instructors at the Radio Advertising Bureau's School for Radio Account Executives. He offered his hand to me.

"Harvey Greene. Pleased to meet you."

"Likewise," I countered, with a firm handshake. He gestured for me to sit in one of the chairs in front of his desk. I sat down and looked around the wood-paneled room. On one wall was a "Miami, See It Like a Native" poster that contained a photograph of a half-naked girl. The poster had been part of a 1970s' advertising campaign designed to depict Miami as a sexy vacation destination. I recalled that it had been the subject of controversy. Miami old-timers had protested the use of a sexy woman representing *their* Miami, or as they called it *"Me-am-ah."* He also displayed an assortment of plaques and awards on the wall and on the credenza behind his desk.

"So you want to come to Miami and sell time on our station?" Harvey asked. "What makes you think you have the stuff to sell WBSG?" *Now that I've seen the place, what makes you think that I want to work here?*

I proceeded to tell him all about my experience. "I earned a bachelor's degree in marketing from Bryant University in

Rhode Island, worked as an on-air deejay in Providence, graduated from the Radio Advertising Bureau's School for Radio Account Executives, and have worked the past nine months as an account executive at WDAR in Providence," I quickly replied, figuring he'd appreciate a quick synopsis during his hectic morning.

As I was finishing, Harvey's phone rang. He lit a cigarette and picked up the receiver. Suddenly Bill leaned over and said, "Let's go!" As we walked out of his office, I wondered what had just happened. How could Harvey have been so abrupt and insincere?

Bill and I walked down the hall to the elevator, and he said, "Thanks for coming, Rick. We don't have an open slot at the moment but stay in touch." *Are you kidding? I'd rather stay in Rhode Island!*

As we waited for the elevator door to open, he handed me his business card and shook my hand. The doors opened, and I heard him say "Good luck."

"Thanks," I replied, as the elevator doors closed.

I had read about the good-guy, bad-guy routine, but these guys ran it to perfection. *It's only part of the game, and I've gained some useful experience in gamesmanship.* I made my way out through the station lobby, said good-bye to the receptionist, and walked out the front door of WBSG. The day hadn't started out well, but it hadn't lessened my enthusiasm to find a radio home in Miami.

Chapter 6

LUNCHING ON LAS OLAS

After starting Ron's car, I checked my watch. It was 11:45 a.m., and my interview at WAXY wasn't until 2:00 p.m. in Fort Lauderdale, a thirty-five-minute drive from downtown Miami.

Ron had told me that Las Olas Boulevard was a Fort Lauderdale landmark with upscale shops and outdoor restaurants, so I decided to make it my destination. Hopefully, I'd find a great place to have lunch and do some people watching.

Upon arriving on Las Olas, I parked my car and walked along the boulevard, stopping at The French Café, the first restaurant with outdoor tables. A tall, well-dressed man in standard waiter attire—white shirt, flowery tie, black pants, and black apron—was standing at the front door. He held menus under his arm and acknowledged my presence with a nod.

"Outside table for one," I stated.

"Right this way," he responded, as we walked along the front of the restaurant to a small table with a view of the street.

"The wine list is on the back." He handed the menu to me, and I perused the food rather than the wine on it. *This is not a good time to get a buzz on.*

A waiter came over to my table. I quickly gazed at the menu.

"I'll have the snapper amandine and a small salad," I said.

"Fine choice, sir," he replied.

I turned my attention to people walking along the boulevard. Across the street was a man dressed in a pastel suit with white shoes. Another wore a blue blazer, madras slacks, white shirt, and red tie. A small group of ladies walked by wearing double-knit pantsuits, their perfume wafting as if it were diesel exhaust. *Gross!* The perfume momentarily overcame the pleasant aroma from the entrées of other restaurant customers close by. I speculated that they had spent hours readying for a "girls' day out" luncheon, as their hair was apparently stiffened with large quantities of hair spray. They were all carrying small purses on their arm (one included a needlepoint of a puppy dog).

Across the street, I noticed several younger women who stood out among the elderly. One was wearing a skin-tight top showing off a generous bustline. Her skirt was also hiked up way above her knees. *What a world of difference from Rhode Island. This is more like it!*

The waiter appeared with my lunch.

"Snapper amandine and a small house salad," he said, placing an aromatic plate of food in front of me and the salad bowl to my right.

"Is there anything else I can get for you, sir?" he asked. "Are you certain you wouldn't care for a glass of white wine with your fish?" That was the last thing I wanted. *Please! Get out of my face with the wine suggestion!*

"I think I'm fine, thank you," I said. "Perhaps some other time."

As I began picking through the fresh greens from my salad, a woman with a dog tethered to a leash walked by. The dog sniffed a tree limb four feet from my table. I thought about encouraging her to continue walking along so I might eat without viewing her canine's discharge. As I was about to speak up, her dog continued walking forward.

The fish was delicious. I devoured it and the salad in a short time and still had a few minutes to view the Fort Lauderdale humankind on Las Olas Boulevard. The waiter appeared, and I ordered a cup of coffee and reviewed my upcoming interview at WAXY.

Having listened to the station in Ron's car, many memories were stirred—including entertaining jingles—from the days growing up in West Orange, New Jersey. Something about the energy of the station was intoxicating.

I finished my coffee and signaled for the waiter to bring me the check. It was approaching 2:00 p.m., so I handed the waiter my charge card, and he quickly returned with my check.

"Thanks," he replied, as I handed him back the receipt. "Please come back and try us again. Next time try your fish with a glass of wine."

Sure, you pestering fool, as long as it's on the house!

Chapter 7

WAXY RADIO

WAXY's offices were located on South Andrews Avenue, across the bridge from the heart of downtown Fort Lauderdale. They were easy to spot; a horizontal sign with WAXY 106 was affixed above the front entrance to the building. There were no parking spots on Andrews Avenue, so I drove around to the back and found that the only available spaces were next door in the Broward Yachts brokerage lot. I parked and shut off the Vega's engine. It sputtered and pinged as if it had had enough for the warm day. *I hope this car's not dying on me.*

Entering the back door of the building, I walked a brief distance down a hallway and saw the station on the right. A large "Oldies Radio WAXY-FM" sign hung above the door. Upon opening the door into a small reception area, I noticed gold shag carpeting and paneled walls. *Furry shag carpeting . . . they take this era seriously!*

I announced myself to the receptionist. "I have an appointment with Ken Brown."

She told me to have a seat in a chair upholstered in furry red cloth and then picked up the telephone to use the intercom. "Ken, you have Rick Charnack in the waiting area."

Within a few minutes Ken appeared. He was dressed in a

beige suit and shirt and a brown striped tie. His hair was combed down over his forehead like an early Beatles' mop.

"I'm Ken, Rick. Welcome to WAXY radio."

"Thanks."

I followed Ken to his office, a short walk past a "bullpen" sales area with six desks. Several salespersons stopped their banter for a moment and gave me a quick stare.

"Don't let the sales animals intimidate you, Rick."

"No problem, Ken," I said as we walked into his office. *He should only know how my survival technique had kept me out of jail Saturday night at The Planet!*

Ken told me he had just been promoted to WAXY's local sales manager and had relocated from Boston. His interest in me had peaked when he discovered that I had been working in Rhode Island. It didn't take long for Ken and me to make a connection.

"What type of accounts are you currently working with?" he asked.

"Mostly retail businesses and restaurants," I said, "but I'm flexible."

"Are you flexible with having me work with you to become better at selling radio?"

"Absolutely!" I responded. *Was he kidding? I've been desperate for someone to help me sell commercials, recalling how Carl cared more about lint than mentoring.*

"I run a unique sales department here. I create opportunities—sales packages—for my staff to sell to retail accounts," he continued. "Are you ready to sell new accounts, Rick?"

"Yes, that's all I've been working with in Providence. I'd love to hear more about your training program. Am I going to be making sales calls with you?"

"Absolutely," offered Ken, "that's the best way for you to learn." *You mean you really get out of the office with your sellers?*

My enthusiasm was now "off the charts," and my water consumption from lunch was taking its toll on my bladder.

"Ken, do you mind if I use your restroom?" I inquired.

"Sure," he commented. "It's next to the sales bullpen."

As I walked out of Ken's office, I was feeling elated. What Ken had just described was exactly what I needed from a manager. *This is too good to be true!*

Just past the bullpen was a door marked "Men." Entering the washroom I noticed several carvings on the wood paneling above the urinal. One said "Welcome to redneck radio" and another "WAXY RADIO . . . WHERE OLDIES GO TO DIE." *How amusing.*

When I returned to his office, Ken was on the phone. He quickly hung up when he saw me.

"Give me a second, Rick. I'll be right back."

Ken stood and walked by me into the station hallway. As I was waiting for him to return, I looked around his office and noticed an array of award plaques that he had earned as a salesperson and sales manager. A "Superior Achiever Award" was affixed to the wall directly next to my seat. *He must especially be proud of this one. It's proof that he's a winner!* On a credenza in back of his desk were additional awards in Lucite frames and a large photograph of a woman. I guessed that was his wife. She was dressed in a conservative dress with pearls. *Perfect for Boston.* Ken returned in a huff.

"Sorry about that!" he exclaimed. "Do you have any questions?"

"Yes. What do you pay your salespersons?" I asked.

"Well, Rick, we pay a draw of $250 per week that is guaranteed for the first ninety days We also have a gas trade so that you won't need to buy your own gas."

"What type of accounts would I be calling on?" I asked.

"It's too early to say, but I'd match you up with accounts that will be a good fit for your skills."

"Are you up for a tour of the station?" asked Ken.

"Absolutely," I responded.

For the next hour or so, Ken took me around the station. He showed me a programming studio where 50s and 60s music prerecorded on large reel-to-reel tapes played alternately on six player decks. One of the songs was just ending when a cued jingle sounded: "WAXY 106—Yesterday's Rock 'n Roll."

A production studio door was adjacent to the programming studio. As Ken opened the door, I saw an announcer in front of a mixing console. The room also contained a large microphone hanging over the console, more reel-to-reel tape machines, and "cart" machines that I recognized for transferring commercials for insertion on air. The announcer turned in his chair. "Rick, this is Darrel Clive, our production director," offered Ken. "He's the best in the business at producing great commercials for new advertisers."

"Hi Rick," responded Darrel enthusiastically. "Welcome to WAXY!"

"Not so fast, Darrel," said Ken. "Rick is here interviewing for a sales job."

"It looked as if you were already on board," Darrel responded. "This is a great place to work, so good luck!" *There's that "good luck" again . . . hope it's genuine this time.*

Ken then led me around the station to meet the copywriter, Carol Vee, who had a phone pinned to her ear but smiled while blowing a cigarette ring. He also showed me the office of the general manager, Mark Cole, but his assistant told Ken that Mark was on the phone.

After we had toured the station, we retreated back to his office and sat down. "Rick, I'll be honest with you," Ken began, "I've already had a conversation with Mark, and he's given me the green light to bring you in. Go back to Providence and continue to work until I give you a call in a week or two."

"Sounds great," I responded.

"Thanks for everything, Ken," I said as I pulled out a business card. "I'm looking forward to working here!"

I stood, shook Ken's hand, and walked out of his office and past the bullpen. After I exited the building, I felt my heart drop. The security fences at Broward Yachts were locked with the Vega inside. How embarrassing! I would have to go back to the station and ask for help. Luckily, when I walked back into the reception area, Ken was talking with a salesperson. He stopped his conversation and looked at me.

"Have you a phone I could use?" I asked.

"Yes, you can use the extension by the chair."

"Do you have the number for Broward Yachts?"

"Sure. Are you blocked in by chance?"

"Yes," I replied sheepishly.

Ken and the salesperson laughed.

"This happens all the time. I'll make a call and have the security guard let you out."

"Thanks!"

Chapter 8

RHODE ISLAND ONCE AGAIN

On Ken's recommendation, I flew back to Providence and returned to work on Tuesday. Carl greeted me with his usual sophomoric humor.

"Good trip to the homeland, Rick?" he inquired.

"Sure was," I replied.

"How are those old folks doing in sunny Fort Lauderdale?"

"Just great." *You'd especially love that oldies radio station! Remember "Walking in the Sand" by the Shangri-Las?*

"When you get settled, come into my office. I've got an important message for you," said Carl.

I walked over to my desk, looked down at it, but decided to put off my paperwork. I walked back to Carl's office.

"You wanted to talk?" I inquired.

"Yes. I received a call from one of your largest accounts who wants to have dinner with you tonight. I told him that you'd call to arrange it." Carl handed me a note with the name and phone number of Bud Carlone, the owner of Fink Oil Company.

"I'm giving you a real shot here, Rick. This is a major account that spends big bucks." *If that's the case, why not take your worthless talent with me on the call? I remember Ken's promise to make calls with me.*

I returned to my desk and called Bud. We made plans to

meet at 8:00 p.m. at Giamberti's Restaurant on Federal Hill, a neighborhood filled with Italian restaurants, several of which were purportedly Mafia hangouts. To put forth an air of professionalism for my most important customer, I drove home, cleaned up, and picked out my best blue suit, white shirt, and yellow paisley tie. I dressed and headed for the "Hill."

I arrived at Giamberti's just before 8:00 p.m. and walked into the bar. The restaurant was a throwback to the forties, dark-red cushioned walls, bolstered high-back chairs, booths with burgundy cloth seats, and enormous crystal chandeliers. The room was filled with sharply dressed men sitting at the bar smoking cigarettes and cigars. Several were wearing dark suits, black shirts, white ties and ballooned black hair. *This could be a scene from a mob movie. All we need is a shootout!*

A buxom blonde-haired hostess walked over to me.

"Are you looking for Mr. Carlone?" *How did she know? Do I look that out of place?*

"Yes, I am."

"Mr. Carlone is already seated and asked me to show you to his table. Please follow me."

We walked out of the bar and through the restaurant into the rear dining room. I saw the only single man seated at a table and speculated that it was Bud. He stood as the blonde sauntered over.

"Bud, I'm Rick Charnack. It's a pleasure to meet you!"

"Likewise. Please sit down and have a drink."

While looking up at the hostess he said, "Two scotches, please."

"I've already ordered calamari, Rick," he said. "They've got the best on the 'Hill.'"

"Sounds great."

Bud was a strikingly handsome man. He wore a dark blue suit with off-white pinstripes, a spread-collar white shirt, and lavender tie. His facial features topped his outfit: blue eyes, salt and pepper hair combed back, and a smile out of a Hollywood movie. I guessed his age was mid-forties. *Could he also be a mobster?*

"I'm delighted you could come out on such short notice."

"No problem. I've been eager to meet you for quite some time." *Especially here on "mob hill."*

The drinks arrived, and we spent the next hour getting acquainted.

"So how long have you been in the business?" Bud questioned.

"Almost a year," I replied.

"Well, I'm not accustomed to working with rookies, but Carl spoke highly of you."

"I'm certain that you won't be disappointed, Bud," I confirmed. *Oh . . . so Carl is throwing me to the wolves!*

Bud began telling me about the oil business and that he was a third-generation Carlone to work at Fink Oil. His grandfather had emigrated from Italy and worked in textile mills before being hired by Fink to drive a delivery truck. His dad had worked through the ranks and eventually became sales manager. Bud had followed in Dad's footsteps and eventually acquired the company by "borrowing" money from family friends. *With a family name like Carlone? Money? And just how did he acquire the money?*

I had already finished my first scotch when the waitress arrived with a third round of drinks. I was clearly on my way to a first-class stupor, which might have been Bud's strategy for getting the "young rookie" to make a deal in his favor. While he continued to tell me about his business, we were startled by several loud popping noises emanating from the front of the restaurant. Fearing the worst, I followed the movement of other patrons by hiding under the table while loud screams could be heard in the bar. I glanced up from the floor and saw several men in dark suits running through a rear door.

In a minute or so, after it quieted down, I rose to see if Bud was okay and noticed he had disappeared! I quickly summoned the waitress.

"What happened?" I asked.

"There's been a shooting at the bar! A member of the Sambetti family has been gunned down!"

The Sambettis were Rhode Island's largest Mafia family and well known for their shady business ventures, including waste disposal and racketeering. The *Providence Bulletin* newspaper had recently reported that they had been expanding their territory without regard to other high-profile families. *That's great . . . a Mafia war being acted out in the same restaurant!*

I looked over to Bud's chair and noticed that his overcoat was missing. Had he dashed out the rear door? *Hmmm . . . oil business? Was he the next in line to be gunned down?*

I hastily put down some cash to pay the bill, grabbed my coat, and scooted out the back door.

While searching the parking lot for Bud, I heard sirens wailing in the distance and an assemblage of Federal Hill onlookers. I scoured the rear parking area. No Bud. I walked around to the front of the restaurant. No Bud. I wanted to call out his name but theorized that wouldn't be a good idea if he were connected to the crime. Several police officers had already arrived and were unrolling yellow tape to block the front entrance of the restaurant. I circled around to the back of the building once more. No Bud.

Disappointed over my seeing my largest account fleeing from our important dinner and fearing police questioning about a mobster hit, I located my car and sped off, feeling emotionally depleted and embarrassed about losing my customer as a gunfight ensued. *What would Carl say?* I stopped for a few drinks on the way home to assuage my catastrophic thoughts.

The following morning, as I was listening to the radio while dressing, I heard details of the previous night's shooting. In addition to the gruesome description of the crime scene—more than one person had been killed and the "hit men" were identified as members of a rival family—several onlookers were interviewed. The shooters had entered the bar area with guns drawn and had shot two members in the head execution style, blood spattering on the bar and the mirror behind it.. An onlooker had suffered a heart attack and was taken to Rhode Island Hospital.

"I saw a black limousine pull up and three men jumped out," said a witness. "They ran into the restaurant and, one minute later, came out and sped away."

"There were two men who casually walked into Giamberti's, and I heard shots fired," another witness offered. "I didn't see them come out." *Maybe they walked out of the rear door, with Bud? Was my client somehow involved in the scene?*

My thoughts were whirling as the next news story brought me back to earth.

"An apartment complex in Cranston is waking up to one of its buildings in ashes this morning. Here's Josh Batista with the story."

"The overnight fire occurred at 1011 Dyer Street in the Meadowview Apartments complex in Cranston. According to an eyewitness who called the fire department, she saw flames in a second-floor window followed by glass popping and black smoke billowing from the apartment. Within minutes, flames were leaping up the side of the structure. The Cranston Fire Department arrived and began escorting tenants—in their night-

*clothes—out of the building while firemen doused the intense
fire with water. Remarkably, no injuries were reported. The
cause of the fire is under investigation, but it is presumed it
began in a second-story apartment. This is Josh Batista in
Cranston reporting for WDAR News."*

An apartment fire? In my complex? One would think that
screaming sirens and startled crowd might have penetrated my
sleep!

I quickly finished dressing and stepped outside to see a
smoldering building just 700 feet away. *Why didn't the fire
department knock on my door? Aren't they supposed to protect
neighboring residents?*

I was astonished. Building fires had always created a fear
in me. While growing up in New Jersey, one New Year's Eve
my brother lit candles that started a fire in our kitchen. A fire
truck, sirens blaring, pulled up to our house, and a group of
firemen barged in to put it out. The chilling memory and fire
this close made me shiver. The smell of burnt wood always got
to me. I had seen enough, and so I dashed for my briefcase
and headed to my car.

To make matters worse, when I arrived at the office I
phoned Bud to show my concern. As it turned out, he wasn't
quite as interested in my welfare.

"I can't do business with you," he quipped. "You're bad
luck!"

*Bad luck? I might have been shot to death in a feud at an Ital-
ian restaurant or died in a building fire!*

"Why, Bud, I suggest that we start from scratch and put
this behind us," I responded.

"No way," he said. "I'm superstitious and won't work with
your station unless someone else handles my account."

Here's some bad luck: A week after the restaurant incident,

I learned that an associate sitting at the desk behind me had written a radio advertising order for almost $80,000. As I congratulated him on his sale, I turned to look at the name on the contract. It was none other than—you guessed it—Fink Oil, my "bad luck" dinner guest, the customer who got away!

Any apprehension about a move to Fort Lauderdale quickly vanished, including my confusion about why I had decided to sell radio in Providence and not pursue a job as a radio announcer. Given the experiences of the past several days, such as gunshots blazing at a restaurant, uncertainty over the role my potential client had played in it, a major apartment fire in my complex, and a weekend weatherman turned sales manager, it became clear to me. This was not just bad luck. It was a bad omen! *This is more than enough evidence that I need to split!*

Fortunately my thoughts turned to South Florida and WAXY radio. I was excited about a quick exit from Rhode Island and the attractive future I knew was awaiting me. It couldn't come soon enough.

Chapter 9

FAREWELL, OCEAN STATE

Following the debacle on Federal Hill, and although I lost interest in selling radio in Rhode Island, I continued to make occasional calls on dead accounts. Dead (or inactive) accounts are businesses that are assigned to rookie salespersons because they are no longer spending ad dollars with the station. It always amused me that these most difficult accounts to sell were handed over to the least experienced sellers. *How ironic!*

The Monday following my return to Providence, my phone rang: "Rick, this is Ken Brown in Fort Lauderdale. How soon can you pack up and get down here?"

"It won't take me long, Ken."

"I've carved out a list for you, so the sooner the better."

"Let me finish up here. I can probably leave by Friday and shoot for a Monday start."

"That's fine. Let me know when you're all set. I'm excited you'll be joining the WAXY sales staff."

"So am I." *Actually, I can't wait to get the hell out of here!*

While I was on the phone, Carl's assistant Marilyn, who also worked with salesmen had left a memo on my desk. The sales team had achieved budget for the past three months and a party had been arranged at a local restaurant that was famous for its *"grog"* drinks—oversized rum cocktails. The

44

memo added, "Be prepared to raise your grog glasses and toast our accomplishment."

I was all for the drinking. However, my thoughts had already turned to living in Fort Lauderdale and the idea of partying with Carl and the station turned me off. I decided it was time to tell him that I was leaving, so I walked into his office.

"Carl, I'm leaving the company," I said. "I want to thank you for all of your support, but a position has been offered to me at a radio station in Fort Lauderdale that I can't refuse."

"I'm sorry to hear that, Rick," he responded. "What station?"

"WAXY-FM."

"FM! You're going to sell an FM station! That's absurd. You are better off staying with AM, Rick. FM is never going to make it!"

"I think I'll take my chances, Carl. Besides, my parents have relocated to Fort Lauderdale, and it's where I want to continue my career in radio sales. *Actually I was thinking about commencing my career anywhere other than here with you in Rhode Island.*

"Well," said Carl, "I can tell that you've probably thought this out. However, why don't you come to Buccaneer Steak House tomorrow night for one last fling? You can call it your 'farewell to WDAR' get-together!"

"Okay, " I said reluctantly, "I'll be there."

I left the office early, and on the way home I stopped at a U-Haul store to purchase boxes to pack my sparse belongings. Along with my two suitcases, boxes, and assorted furnishings, I speculated that there would be plenty of room in my Volvo. The following day everyone at the office cleared out at noon to prepare for the party. I used my free time to pack.

Arriving at the party shortly after 7:00 p.m., I was greeted by Les Pell. Les was the elder statesman of the sales team who had recently endured a miserable divorce and was an emotional wreck. I felt so sorry for Les that on several occasions I'd accepted his luncheon invitations, during which he'd sob uncontrollably into a Bloody Mary.

"Heard you're leaving," said Les.

"Yes, I'm moving to Florida."

"That's a good decision, young man. This place is a *has been* in the radio business."

"How are you feeling today, Les?"

"Got a few minutes, Rick?"

"Yes, but I'm trying to get this over with. Let's talk later." I was in no mood to hear the same story that Les had told me a countless number of times.

Carl walked over with a sharply dressed young man at his side.

"Rick, this is Ben Sheppard. He's with our national sales rep organization, Pro Radio."

"Nice to meet you, Rick. I heard you're moving to Fort Lauderdale to work for WAXY."

"Right."

"I thought you might like to know that I represent a new FM station in your market, Y100, that will soon become the top-rated station in Fort Lauderdale. Their slogan is "Don't say hello—say I listen to the new sound of Y100 and win one thousand dollars."

"Great. Sounds like fair competition."

"Fair competition, Rick? Their promotional budget exceeds one million dollars!" *Holy crap . . . perhaps I need to rethink my move to WAXY.*

He turned to Carl, and they both laughed.

Carl said, "You're certain you want to leave, Rick?"

"Yes, and good luck, Ben. It's nice to have met you." *I'll take my chances at WAXY with Ken as my mentor.*

I looked around at the crowd for the last time. Wendy, the station copywriter who had been eyeing me the entire evening walked in my direction. It appeared that she was no longer interested in the party and had other things on her mind. She stood in front of me and blurted out, "Would you like more private company for the remainder of the evening?"

"How many grogs have you had, Wendy?"

"Enough to follow my primal instincts."

"Let's hang out for the awards and afterward meet me at the coat check."

"Done."

Wendy had been someone whose not-so-discreet flirting with me at the station didn't go unnoticed. Along with her copywriting skills, she had excellent looks to match. She was petite—about five feet, one inch—with short, dyed blonde hair with bangs and a cute angular face with a constant wide smile and great teeth, a rarity in Providence. Her years in an orthodontist's chair had clearly paid off. What stood out most was her proclivity to dress in a highly coquettish manner— always a short skirt, leather boots, and revealing cleavage.

Eventually, Carl stood before us and presented awards to the sellers who had exceeded their quarterly budget. I was happy for Jay Hunt, my college friend who was singled out for his performance. I walked over to him following the announcement of his award.

"Congratulations, Jay," I said. "It won't be long until you're running the sales department."

"Thanks, Rick. But that douchebag is safe as long as we continue to make our budgets. We're successful despite Carl."

"I know. He's been of no help whatsoever to me. I need to find a manager who can help me learn the ins and outs of selling radio, and I think I've found one in Fort Lauderdale."

"I completely understand. Next time we speak, you'll be

kicking ass in Fort Lauderdale. Call me if I can ever be of help."

"Thanks, Jay."

A final presentation was made by Sid Reed, Sr., director of sales, to honor Carl for his excellence in management. *Oh boy. This is pathetic!* Following his "acceptance" speech, which contained mostly undistinguishable slurred words—*What a surprise!*—I walked over and thanked Carl for hiring me and said I was going to "stay in touch." *Only if hell freezes over!*

The emotions I was feeling were mixed. On one hand I felt saddened that I was leaving the first "real" radio company I had worked for, but on the other I was feeling giddy about my relocation to sunny South Florida. The two "grogs" I had downed didn't hurt either. Wendy, whom I had told to meet me at the coat check, was waiting for me, coat in hand.

"Ready?" I asked.

"Are you kidding? I've been ready since you first walked into the station."

"Then let's get away from this madness," I said, as we exited Buccaneer Steak House.

* * *

The following morning, after Wendy had left my place, I called the station to say good-bye to Carl's assistant , Marilyn. Although she tried to help me with proposals and correspondence, her work had been untenable. Case in point: She had once mailed contracts to several wrong customers on my list! Unfortunately, everyone put up with her because Carl loved it when she laughed, hysterically, at his pathetic jokes.

"Take care, Marilyn," I offered.

"You, too, Rick. Don't be a stranger." *Right, I'll keep that in mind!*

I finished packing my belongings, which included mostly

clothes. The furniture had been rented, and I confirmed a pickup for the following morning. That evening I drove to a nearby restaurant that had bartered with the station. I sat at the bar and ordered the most expensive steak on the menu, giant salad, and Narragansett beer. The bar's television was tuned to a Boston Bruins hockey game, and lots of hoopla could be heard radiating from the large crowd that was fixated on the screen. As I finished my dinner and rose to leave the bar, I noticed that the Bruins were down 4 to 1 to the New York Rangers. *And, yet, another good omen about leaving New England?*

The following day, Able Furniture Rental employees arrived shortly after 10:00 a.m. and quickly moved out the living room and bedroom furniture. When they finished, I stopped at the rental office to return my key and wished Kay Wishom, the rental director, farewell. She had allowed me an early lease termination because of the long waiting list at Meadowbrook Apartments.

I returned to my apartment, took one last look around, shut the door and walked to my packed Volvo. I drove to the I-95 south ramp and onto the highway. A quick glance in my rearview mirror revealed the fading skyline of Providence. *It was just as I had dreamed.*

Chapter 10

APPLE HOMES

Upon my arrival in South Florida, I spent a week sleeping on the pullout sofa in my parents' apartment. Following seven nights of restless sleeping, I decided that it was time to find a permanent home in the Fort Lauderdale area. WAXY'S receptionist informed me that she had a friend, Ron Kaub, who was looking to share a two-bedroom apartment. I called Ron and made arrangements to meet him for breakfast on Saturday morning.

Ron had moved to Fort Lauderdale so he could work and go to college evenings and weekends for his master's degree. *Perfect . . . I'll have the place to myself most of the time!*

"What are you looking for?" I asked Ron, as the waitress refilled our coffee mugs.

"Just a place to rest my head," he replied.

"Do you have any other specific needs?"

"Not really, I'm very low-key and won't be using the apartment for partying, if that concerns you. I just need a place to study some nights, but I'm certain I can shut the door to my room if you have company." *Perfect . . . the invisible roommate!*

After spending a few more hours with Ron, we seemed to be in similar circumstances in our lives: launching careers and adapting to the South Florida lifestyle. We decided to begin our search for a two-bedroom apartment in the *Fort Lauderdale News*. After reviewing the ads, we discovered a new apartment complex that had originally been built as condominiums and featured oversized rooms and plenty of space. Because the market for condo sales had softened, the units had been converted to rentals.

We drove over to see the apartment and signed a lease on the spot. I spent the remainder of the weekend furniture shopping and moving my belongings into the apartment.

For the first several weeks, while I acclimated to Fort Lauderdale, my enthusiasm was high. The stations' oldies format was to my liking, customers seemed open to my ideas about reaching WAXY's audience, and Ken worked with me on my selling skills. My first sale was to a Buick dealership that included premium rates for morning newscasts. When I submitted the contract, Ken told me that I had "overcharged" the customer.

"What?" I asked incredulously.

"You can't charge that much for our morning drive time," explained Ken.

"But the customer's willing to pay for it! I sold it for a premium. Isn't our airtime worth it?"

"Sure, but let's charge the normal rate and give him more spots in other time periods."

"Fine."

I found it hard to believe that I had made a sale at premium rates that weren't acceptable. In my brief experience in Rhode Island, our station charged more for premium time slots, such as newscasts. *Could selling be this different in Florida?* I adjusted the contract and called my customer with the good news. He was very appreciative. *He better be. He just received free ads!*

At our Monday morning sales meetings, Ken introduced new sales packages designed to appeal to new prospects. They included everything from rate discounts to weekend music-themed sponsorships. I took several copies of each package to present to new and existing customers and began to recognize that selling radio was a profession of psychedelic highs and unwelcomed crashes (not minor highs and lows) based on my latest sale. What's more, my feelings of self-worth were often linked to my most recent sale.

An example of how I took out my frustration happened with a potentially large customer. I had originally identified this new target, Apple Homes, by tearing out a large, full-page ad in the *Fort Lauderdale News*. The customer consistently bought full pages, which were very expensive, so I sensed that his advertising budget was large.

I theorized that WAXY's audience of twenty-five- to thirty-five-year-olds, those first-time homebuyers who were traditionally not newspaper readers, was a perfect target for him. Following several failed attempts to reach the owner by telephone, I eventually connected with him by stopping by his office. Jerry Hershon, a heavy-set, midget-sized man who wore dark glasses and madras slacks, walked out from his secluded office to meet me.

"You're very fortunate to have broken through my media wall," Jerry said. "You are the most persistent salesperson I've ever met!"

"I believe in my station."

"Well, I've broken ground on a community that appeals to younger families. Come into my office and I'll tell you about it."

Surprisingly, Jerry was remarkably glib and provided me with information about the big plans for the company's new community of modestly priced homes that would appeal to first time buyers. *WAXY's target audience!* He also felt comfortable enough to share his life story in the building business and tales about his family. I took great interest when he told me it was his first venture into the younger market. *This is my chance to land a HUGE contract!*

Boosting my hopes for a successful outcome, he asked me to return as soon as possible with a proposal and sample commercial from WAXY's production department. "I'm glad you persisted in getting to me, Rick, and I admire your ambition." He added, "Don't worry. Your time will be rewarded. Bring back a proposal for $25,000 and one for $30,000." *Okay . . . tell me this isn't another full-of-crap advertiser!*

Following a chance meeting with an elusive prospect, I spent the next several evenings working on the proposal and a sample commercial with Darrel Clive, WAXY's production manager. Darrel made up for his lean talent with a willingness to help sellers by working late hours to create sample commercials (or "spec spots," as they were called).

I spent Sunday finishing up the proposal and felt certain that Darrel's effort would impress Jerry and, ultimately, make the sale. On Monday afternoon, I drove over to Apple Homes, walked into the offices with my briefcase and a cassette player with which to play the sample commercial, and confidently approached the receptionist. Introducing myself once again, I asked for Jerry and was astonished at what she told me.

"We've decided we aren't doing any more advertising at the moment," she said. "I know you were supposed to see him, but I have strict instructions *not* to allow any media sellers, especially you radio people. We *don't* like radio and *don't ever* want to use it, so *please leave.*"

I was shocked! After all, hadn't this prospect told me that my ambition would be rewarded? And, having been in a sales slump for eight days, my self-worth and commission payout were directly tied to a successful outcome.

I felt humiliated, having spent hours preparing the proposal and sample commercial. *I worked on this as if it were my own company!*

What were my options? I could say "thank you," leave the building, go straight to my car, close the windows, turn up the radio, and scream several obscenities at "midget man." Or I could make a statement that wouldn't be very appropriate in the emotional condition I was in. *Better calm down before you do something stupid!*

I suddenly felt intense heat inside my body erupting into my head. My better judgment fell by the wayside. I impulsively blurted out, "Tell that madras midget to get his fat ass out here, right now," I said. "I'm not here to take any more of your nonsense, so get up and fetch him, right now!"

As the last of these words crossed my lips, I immediately recognized the ills of my behavior. Clearly this wasn't the way professionals acted, even during a bad sales cycle. All of the tools I had learned, all my sales training, went out the window. All of the testosterone that had been built up in my brain had short-circuited in an instant. Just then I heard the patter of feet coming from Jerry's office.

"Get out!" he shouted, "Get out of my offices right now!"

"What happened, Jerry?" I responded. "I thought you were determined to reach our audience! And I've brought a custom proposal and sample commercial that was prepared especially for your new development!"

"I don't care if you give it to me for free!" he countered. "It's my prerogative to change my mind if I so choose. Now get the hell out of here before I call the police!"

It didn't take me long to realize I had better scoot, or be

scooted, so I retreated, tail between my legs and out the door to my car.

To relieve the pain, I drove to a nearby convenience store and treated myself to an ice cream sandwich and several candy bars, the most readily available comfort food. It relieved the pain, if only temporarily. *What was I thinking? I could get fired for this!*

Chapter 11

ATONEMENT?

Back at the office, upon entering the sales "pit," I was greeted by WAXY's general manager, Mark Cole. Mark was a burly, homegrown California "fella" who had made it big in the sixties at Los Angeles's top-rated hit radio station. He was also a guy who drank Bushmills and had permanent yellow stains on his fingers from a lifetime of smoking Pall Malls. What Mark was doing running a radio station in cosmopolitan Miami was beyond me. He suggested I spend a few minutes in his office with him.

After lighting a Pall Mall and having his secretary, Suzanne, bring him a cup of black coffee, he turned to me.

"I understand you had a tough sales call at Apple Homes," he said. "They called me right after you left their offices." *No doubt midget man had done a fine job of trashing my sales approach, potentially derailing my fledgling sales career. Am I getting fired?*

"Rickkker," Mark grunted, inhaling a fresh drag from his smoke, "I can't say that I haven't done the same thing in my selling days." And, as punctuation, he bellowed out "Haaaah, haaaah!"

"You know, Rickkker, we can't win on every sales call. And, we certainly can't tell these assholes how we really feel!

Haaaah, haaaah!" Mark continued, "I think you're a little tense, aren't you Rickkkerrooo? I've got just the thing for you."

"What?" I curiously responded, as he tapped the ashes from the Pall Mall with his fat yellow fingers. "Do you want me to take a leave of absence?"

"Haaaah, haaaah," answered Mark. "No, I'm thinking you need a visit to WAXY's therapist!" *Okay . . . where's he going with this? I'm not a candidate for a shrink!*

I was suddenly feeling more confused and humiliated than at any time during that tumultuous day. How was a shrink going to help me turn around my current sales slump? Based on the current circumstances, however, I had no choice, so I took the easy way out, the authentic "suck up" method.

"Sure," I said, "if you think it would do me some good."

"Do you some good?" he bellowed. "It will fix you right up, haaaah, haaaah."

With that said, he pressed the intercom button and spoke into it.

"Pam, can you come in here, please?"

Pam was the station business manager who kept the books and wrote all of the company checks. I wondered why he would be calling her in. In a matter of moments, she poked her head into his office.

"Yes?" she inquired.

After puffing on the last bit of his Pall Mall and putting it out in a giant silver ashtray, he looked up at her, smiling.

"Rickkker here needs to visit Dominic Comici, so make out a check for seventy-five dollars."

"Sure," she said. "I'll be right back."

As Pam turned to leave Mark's office, I could swear I heard her snicker. And as soon as she returned with the check for his signature, I gave Pam a sheepish smile. Following Mark's advice to?" pack up and leave immediately for my "appointment" with Dominic Comici, I slipped into the Volvo and retrieved the directions that I had scribbled down in his office. What seemed unusual was that a shrink's office was located in the penthouse of a North Miami high-rise apartment building.

When I arrived, no "guest" spaces were available in front or on the side of the building, so I drove to the next block and squeezed my Volvo between a Camaro and an Oldsmobile Toronado. I walked up to the front entrance of the building and pressed the button next to "Comici" on the phone directory.

"Yes," came a female voice through the speaker.

"Mark Cole set an appointment for me."

"Oh, yes, come right up to the penthouse level, and I'll meet you by the elevator." A buzzer on the front door allowed me to enter into the building. I walked into the lobby, which was furnished in early 1970s wood-and-mirrors décor. Several wilted floor plants framed the building elevator. I stepped into the elevator, pressed the "P," and straightened my tie as the elevator made its way to the top floor. What happened next can only be described as *amazing*.

Standing outside the elevator doors was a barefooted woman, mid-thirties, dressed in a negligée. She was roughly five feet, three inches tall, with shoulder-length black hair, a busty but trim figure, and great legs—overall a very hot body. Her smile was entirely inviting. Walking off the elevator, I was convinced that she was waiting for someone else. Then she spoke.

"Rick?" she asked. "I'm Stacy. Mark told me to expect you. Why don't you come this way so that we can get started."

"Get started?" I asked. "I think there's been a mistake."

"No mistake," she countered. "Mark briefed me. He told me that you were in need of a 'session.'"

Stacy led me down the hall and through an open apartment door. She suggested that I relax on the couch while she brought me a drink. The apartment was fairly large, with an outside terrace that might have been beautiful had there been any live vegetation or plants on it. Instead, I noticed empty planter pots, a small table and chairs and a view of North Miami and Biscayne Bay that was terrific. I had the distinct impression that most of the sessions were held indoors.

"Rick," came Stacy's voice as she walked back into the room with a drink in one hand and what appeared to be a stunning young woman in the other, "this is Cindy. She will be in charge of your session."

Cindy appeared to be a very young, almost nubile teenager. She was wearing a pale blue see-through negligee. She had light brown hair that curled down past her shoulders and rested halfway down her back.

"Here's your drink," Stacy offered. "Let me explain how we conduct our therapy sessions. First of all, you *are aware* of our total discretion here, right?"

"Sure," I said, trying to look discreetly at Cindy's glorious bust.

"Well, since this is your first time, I think you ought to know our policies. We specialize in *servicing* the media here. Our fees are $75 per session. Do you have the check with you?"

"Yes, here it is," I responded, removing the check from my pocket and handing it over to Stacy.

"By the way," I asked. "What type of therapy do you offer?"

With a loud giggle that reverberated throughout the penthouse, Cindy commented, "Rick, please come with me."

She took my hand and led me into another room in the apartment. The "session room" turned out to be a bedroom featuring floor-to-ceiling mirrors surrounding a king-size bed.

Cindy pulled the negligée over her head so as not to hide anything from me, looked at me, and exclaimed, "Let's start the session, Rick."

As I prepared for my session with WAXY's "shrink," I reflected on a truly amazing day. First, I had torched a prospective customer with disparaging remarks. Then I had consumed several candy bars and an ice cream sandwich to assuage my guilt over it. While fearful that I might lose my job, I was called into the general manager's office, and, finally, he had sent me to relieve my stress with a beautiful young girl in a penthouse apartment.

If this was the type of experiences that radio sales were about, and if the punishment for vocalizing my displeasure with a prospective customer would result in a "shrink" session of sex with a teenage-looking girl, I'd be proud to make certain it happened again. *Very soon.*

Chapter 12

THE JINGLE MAN COMETH

If you were an avid radio listener or television viewer in the 1950s or 1960s, you probably remember slogans like "See the USA in your Chevrolet" or "Winston tastes good like a cigarette should." These catchy tunes were whistled, even sung out loud, and used to brand products indelibly in our memory.

In the 1970s, as advertising agencies began to pull away from using jingles in their clients' advertising, large jingle companies (or "houses" as they were called) found it necessary to more proactively solicit business, even send out "jingle salesmen" to assist radio stations in pitching local advertisers to use them. The premise was a good one: In exchange for a radio schedule purchase, the station would provide the client a jingle at no extra charge.

I heard about these jingle salesmen. They were in a class by themselves, usually identifiable by their disheveled look, and they—in WAXY's case, Martin Landy—would typically blow into town to help the sales team assemble a list of prospects and make sales calls. And Martin didn't disappoint. He showed up in creased khaki slacks, a button-down, faded, blue-striped shirt and hush puppies. Upon a closer look, several buttons from his blazer were missing.

Having worked at WAXY for about nine months, my list was still fairly small, so I could only identify two with enough ad dollars to warrant a presentation.

Several weeks prior to the arrival of "jingle man," I had set an appointment with my sales manager, Ken, to see Bob Kane, the Regional Director for Sweden House, a smorgasbord-style restaurant. The restaurants throughout Florida were famous for their tall blonde waitresses and bountiful buffet offerings.

Following the call, we both felt it went extremely well. Ken had hit on the regional director's love for W. C. Fields after noticing a bust of him on a credenza.

"I never met a kid I liked," chirped Ken in his best W. C. Fields imitation.

"It's morally wrong to allow a sucker to keep his money," Bob responded, laughing.

This went on for several minutes. The client eventually told us that there wasn't anything planned for radio at the moment but he had big plans for the near future.

"Great," I said. "When can I get back to you?"

"Call me next month," Bob responded.

This was the type of response that's a put-off to get you out of a customer's office. However, as soon as we left, both Ken and I felt that Bob would live up to his word. Ken also suggested that I purchase a W. C. Fields album and drop it off the following day as a show of appreciation for Bob's time.

"If you leave it with his receptionist, it's as good as making a sales call," he said, "and it will leave a lasting impression."

A few weeks later, Martin Landy arrived at the station in his frumpy attire and assembled the sales team in the conference room to map out his schedule. He had been given a list of accounts to target.

"Who's got Sweden House?" he asked.

"I do," I replied.

"Great. Restaurants are ideal target for jingles." *Perfect . . .
I hope W. C. Fields will give us an advantage.*

I contacted Bob Kane to set up an appointment, and the following day we made a sales call at Sweden House to a welcoming client. It turned out that he had been talking to all of the Florida franchisees about using radio, and a jingle might be the perfect way to get their commitment.

"I've been pitched by so many radio sellers that I probably know radio's benefits by heart," he said. "I'm sold on using it and would love for you to present it at the next franchise meeting."

"When is it?"

"In three weeks. Can the jingle be finished by then?"

"Absolutely," Martin said. "I'll put a rush on it."

"There's only one obstacle," said Bob Kane. "The meeting is in Cocoa Beach. Do you think you can make the trip?"

"No problem," I said. "I'll be there." *Did I really just commit to make a six-hour road trip?*

We spent the next hour or so collecting important factual information that would be germane to making a jingle. At the end of the Q & A session, he told us to have dinner at his Fort Lauderdale location.

"Here are two passes," he said. "Dinner's on me."

"Thanks," I said. "We'll finish up our research, and I'll be in touch in a week or so. In the meantime, rest assured you'll have a great jingle to share with all of the franchisees."

"I've got confidence in your station, Rick," he replied.

"One last thing, Bob," I told him. "The package requires your airtime commitment to WAXY for eighteen thousand dollars to air over a six-month period. We can work out the schedule details once it's approved, okay?"

"I'm not worried about the money, Rick. Just get me a great Sweden House jingle."

Once again, I left our meeting feeling extremely optimistic. Later than evening, Martin and I ate dinner at the Fort Lauderdale Sweden House.

"Food's tasty," he said, wiping gravy from his chin. "I'll make certain to give my creative people some great information after this terrific meal!" *Sure you will. I suppose you want to take some "to go"?* "Give me about two weeks, and I'll send you the completed jingle."

"Wow!" I said. "That's fast. Bob will be very impressed."

"Impressing clients is what we're all about."

I smiled. *Only a jingle salesman could sound so insincere!*

When we returned from the sales call, Mark Cole called Martin into his office. Within a few minutes, I was summoned into the meeting.

"Nice job, Rickkkerrooo!" Mark grunted, after blowing a smoke ring from his Pall Mall cigarette. "Seems as if you've got the best track on selling a jingle!"

"Looks that way," I responded. "With the client on our team, it looks good. The only challenge is getting to Cocoa Beach and back, but I'd be happy to make the drive."

"No way, Rickkkerrooo. You've got better things to do than spend six hours on the road. Besides we have a trade-out with an air charter service."

"Great," I responded. *A small airplane? Flying in the summer storms? Is this guy nuts?*

Mark turned to Martin. "Okay, let's get back to work. I'll handle the travel details, and you make certain the jingle gets done on time."

"No problem. You can count on me!" responded Martin. *What a ham!*

Two weeks went by, and my phone rang.

"Hi, Rick. It's Martin Landy here in Dallas. I've got something ready for you to listen to."

"Great," I responded. "Let me hear it."

"Okay."

I overheard some background noise. It sounded like he was talking with a production engineer readying the jingle to play over the phone. Suddenly a burst of music: *"Sweden House, smorgasbord, all you want for just one price! Sweden House, smorgasbord, all you want for just one price!"*

"What do you think?" he inquired.

"Just okay." I said. *Actually, it's pretty lame, but what do I know about jingles?* "You *are* going to finish the song, right?"

"Of course. I just wanted you to hear the refrain for now."

We made arrangements for the final mix to be sent by early the following week. My trip and presentation were scheduled for Thursday, so I had planned an extra day to finish up the proposal. Shortly after the call, I contacted Bob Kane with the good news.

"I just heard your jingle," I said. "It sounds great!"

"Okay," Bob said. "Remember, our meeting next Thursday at 11 a.m. at Sweden House on U.S. 1 in Cocoa Beach."

"No problem, Bob. I've made travel arrangements to be there by 11 a.m. sharp." I walked over to Ken's office and shared with him the latest developments.

"Let's go and see Mark," he said. "We need to discuss the air arrangements."

"Fine," I said. *Just hearing the word air started to make me feel queasy.*

We walked into Mark's office and made ourselves comfortable in his chairs.

"Okay, Rickkkerrooo, here's the plan."

For the next several minutes, Mark explained the details of my flight to Cocoa Beach. I was to check in at the Tropical Airways terminal at 9:00 a.m. The terminal was located on the south end of the Fort Lauderdale-Hollywood Airport.

"Just ask for Hal when you arrive at the terminal. He's our contact and will take care of everything." *Ask for Hal? Is this a secret code? Do I need a password?*

"Fine," I said. "But you are certain that he knows I'm coming, right, Mark?"

"Sure does, Rickkkerrooo. Have a great trip and good luck with Sweden House!"

The following Thursday I arrived at the station at 8:00 a.m. to collect the tapes.

I had made thirteen copies so that each franchisee had one to take back to his local market. I took a cassette player with me—the largest I could find—so that I could play the jingle for all to hear during my presentation.

In 1974, the Fort Lauderdale-Hollywood airport was a far cry from what it is today. At that time the terminals were single-story buildings that offered passengers entry and exit from aircraft via portable staircases that were rolled onto the tarmac. Just east of the airport runway was a drive-in movie theater where planes would often come roaring over the top of the theater screen. I remember spending an evening at the drive-in with a date and each time a plane would roar overhead, I'd hear static coming through the portable speakers. Unless you were attending a horror movie, frequent attendance at the Airport Drive-in was limited for fear of a passenger airliner colliding with the screen. *What a nightmare!*

I circled around past the commercial airline area to an entrance on the south side of the airport where I looked for the Tropical Airways building. I entered through a gate and immediately noticed several private planes on the tarmac directly in front of a double-wide trailer. A small *Tropical Airways* sign was affixed to the trailer above the entry door.

I parked my car and walked over to the entrance and up

two stairs to the front door. I opened the door and looked inside to find dimly lit offices. I walked in.

"Hal here?" I asked hesitantly.

"Sure is," responded a voice from behind the counter at the far end of the building. "Hal's my name, flying airplanes is my game!" *Oh no, this can't be . . . I'm going to die!*

"You must be Rick," he said. "You're right on time. I just fueled up the plane we'll be taking to Cocoa Beach."

"Great. How long will it take to get there?"

"About an hour, give or take fifteen minutes. As soon as I've completed my flight plan, we'll get going." Hal then emerged from behind the counter. His "captain's outfit" amounted to jean shorts and flip-flops, and I could see that he was walking with a distinct limp.

"I see you've a limp, Hal," I said.

"A war injury," he replied. He then pulled on a cap he was wearing with "Girls Fly Free" embroidered on it.

"You can load up now," he said. "The cargo door's open."

I walked outside and saw the airplane directly in front of me. It was a small, twin-engine white aircraft with yellow and green stripes. A plastic milk crate sat next to the right door. Any small amount of confidence I had been feeling was quickly diminished upon viewing the crate. *Nice staircase! Is this what they mean when they say "going the extra mile" to make a sale?*

A small hatch door was open near the airplane's tail. I walked over and placed my briefcase and cassette player inside the compartment and buckled them down with straps.

"Ready?" Hal asked from behind me.

"I'm ready," I said. *As I'll ever be.*

I climbed onto the milk crate, slipped into the passenger seat, and closed the door. I was less than impressed with the door's "clang" rather than a more solid "thud" like my car door.

Hal removed the crate, walked around the plane, and jumped into his seat. He started the engines, which were so loud we couldn't hear each other, and the plane bucked back and forth. Hal then steered the plane forward, and the plane began taxiing to the runway.

He motioned to me to put on a pair of headphones that were lying next to my seat. After putting them on, I could barely discern him communicating with the tower. Most of it was unintelligible. After a few minutes of navigating the taxiways, he throttled the engines, we gathered speed on the main runway, and before long we were airborne.

He then turned to me and said, "See those clouds beginning to form?"

"Yes."

"We need to be careful that we return before the afternoon thundershowers pile high on the peninsula, or else it will be a bumpy ride home."

"Great," I said. "How bumpy will it get?"

"Let's just say you might need a barf bag." *Great. Can we turn around now?*

Hal began to point out landmarks on the ground. I took one look down and almost lost my breakfast as we passed over highrise condominiums (that the plane seemed to almost touch).

Upon further examination, I viewed ocean waves breaking on the beachfront where tiny specs of humankind were apparently walking. It was all too much for me to observe, so I stared forward, checking out the gauges. I was becoming drowsy from the drone of the engines and managed to fall into a light sleep. It seemed like a short time before I heard Hal jabbering with the Cocoa Beach tower.

"We're on our descent and will be on the ground in ten minutes," he told me. I looked at my watch and saw that it was only 10:15 a.m.

"Great," I gasped. *That gives me plenty of time to get out of this death trap and to my presentation.*

Shortly after landing and taxiing to a small building, Hal cracked a window on his side and a rush of hot air came swirling into the plane.

"Warm day here in Cocoa," he said. "Remember what I said about getting out of here no later than one o'clock."

"No problem." *I'll just rush the presentation so that I don't die on the way home.*

I disembarked by jumping down, opened the cargo door, and unloaded my briefcase and cassette player. There was a taxi at the end of the building.

"I should be back at one o'clock," I explained, regaining my footing and walking toward the taxi.

The taxi driver opened my door and asked me where I was headed.

"Sweden House."

"Which one?"

"You're telling me there's more than one?"

"Yep. There's one in South Cocoa and another just up the coast."

"The only one in Cocoa Beach is in South Cocoa, right?"

"That's right."

"Well, take me there."

A half-hour later we pulled into the Sweden House parking lot. A dozen or so cars were parked in front, and since it wasn't the lunch hour yet, I guessed the cars were owned by the franchisees.

"Okay," I told the taxi driver. " Can you be here at twelve-thirty sharp?"

"No problem."

I dug into my pocket for my wallet, paid the driver, and stepped out to retrieve my briefcase and cassette player. I wobbled toward the restaurant door. *Great. Now I've got a case of vertigo. Whose idea was this airplane trip?*

As soon as I stepped into the restaurant, I heard voices coming from the dining area. When I came within sight of Bob Kane, he rose from his chair and came around to meet me.

"Are you all set?" he said. "I'm going to introduce you in five minutes or so."

"Fine," I replied, looking at my watch. *May I have a glass of club soda?*

Bob returned to the head of the table and continued to conduct the group's business.

I reviewed my brief presentation. I then peered around the restaurant. The walls were painted pale blue and trimmed with yellow. A long buffet counter hid behind a lattice wall. I remember someone telling me that the two most appealing colors at restaurants were red and yellow, like McDonald's. I wondered how anyone could conjure up an appetite while looking at faded blue walls. However, Sweden House was a successful business, and that was all that mattered. I turned to face Bob Kane as he walked toward me.

"Ready?" he asked.

"Absolutely!" We walked over to the group, and he asked for their attention.

"Ladies and gentlemen, I told you that I had some exciting news about a new advertising program. I would like to introduce a representative from WAXY Radio in Fort Lauderdale, the radio station that I've chosen to kick off my new campaign. Rick Charnack has flown up here for you to preview the Sweden House "jingle" that I think you're going to love! Rick, the floor's yours."

I peered at the U-shaped table.

"Thank you, Bob, for the opportunity to showcase radio

in an entirely different light." I handed out folders that contained a few pages of radio research along with cassette-tape copies of the Sweden House jingle. Several of the franchisees began talking among themselves with alternating looks at me.

"What's in it for us?" someone asked.

"New customers," I replied.

"Can you guarantee it?"

Bob spoke up. "You'll have plenty of time to weigh your options. I propose you keep an open mind and just listen for now. Rick, go ahead."

"Okay," I said, plugging in my boom box. I went ahead and launched into my "See the USA in your Chevrolet" pitch, highlighting the benefits of using music to stir emotion in prospective customers. I also spoke about radio's enormous reach potential—approximately 95 percent of the population each week—and how it could assist Sweden House to bring in new customers. When I was finished, I turned to the boom box and played the jingle:

"Sweden House, smorgasbord, all you want for just one price! Sweden House, smorgasbord, all you want for just one price!" An instrumental portion followed next. I lowered the music.

"This is where your local station announcer will provide specifics such as specials, locations, and directions." I raised the volume.

"Sweden House, smorgasbord, all you want for just one price! Sweden House, smorgasbord . . . oh so good!" I looked around the room. Many were smiling and wanted to hear it again. I quickly rewound the tape and replayed the jingle. When it ended, Bob stood up and applauded.

"Well, folks, you can see why Rick came all the way here from Fort Lauderdale." *That's it? A ten minute meeting and I'm done?* He's brought copies for all to take back to your markets. Let's thank Rick." A less than thunderous round of applause spread through the room. I collected my things, and Bob led me to the front of the restaurant.

"Don't worry about their reaction," he said. "They are all die-hard newspaper fans who are set in their ways. All they need to hear is the great job radio is doing in Fort Lauderdale and they'll hop on board. *Great job radio is doing. . . . Does that mean I have a deal?* Bob held his hand out to shake mine.

"We have a deal. Stop by on Monday, and we'll work out the details of our schedule."

"Thanks, Bob," I said. "I appreciate your confidence."

"Thank you, Rick," he said, "for a job well done."

I looked at my watch. It was 12:20 p.m. I walked out the front door and saw the taxi already waiting for me. I jumped in, and the driver confirmed our destination. Realizing that I had just made an $18,000 sale, I rolled down the rear window to do what most media salesmen do upon closing a large order . . . scream!

My sudden enthusiasm, however, was dampened by the thought of flying back to Fort Lauderdale with Hal at the controls. As we drove the streets of Cocoa Beach on the way back to the airport, I tried to ignore the flood of worries that came into my head. Taking deep breaths and repeating sane thoughts helped. *You're going to be fine. You're going to be fine. You'll arrive back in Fort Lauderdale in one piece!*

It wasn't long before I saw signs directing us to the airport. Up ahead the tower came into view. Looking at my watch, I saw that it was only 12:45, which left us plenty of time to make our "getaway." As the taxi pulled up, I noticed Hal talking with a woman in a short skirt, sporting long blonde hair and a low-cut blouse. As I opened the door, I heard them both laughing.

"Why don't you fly home with me?" I overheard Hal say, peering into her eyes.

"You know I'm married, Hal!" she responded.

"Doesn't matter to me."

"I know. It never has." *Shouldn't he be preparing for the flight instead of flirting with a married woman?* Walking from the taxi toward the airplane, I noticed that she was straightening her dress as if she had been caught red-handed. Hal then looked at me and said something about the cargo door. I opened the compartment and, once again, tied down my briefcase and cassette player. Suddenly, I heard a growl coming from my stomach and realized that I hadn't eaten since breakfast. Perhaps I should try to eat something.

"Anywhere I can grab a sandwich?" I asked Hal.

"Don't even think about it!" he shouted.

"Why?"

"I don't have large enough barf bags on board." *Very funny!*

"Okay," I said. "Let's get out of here." I jumped aboard, and after saying good-bye to his lady friend, Hal vaulted into his seat and clicked his seat belt.

"Better make certain yours is snuggly fastened. You may need it!"

"Hal, I've had just about enough of this already!" *You're making me feel sick even before we leave the ground!*

He started the engines and taxied the short distance to the main runway. As we turned to take off to the east, I could see dark thunderclouds rolling in. The airplane jolted into the air. As we ascended into the clouds, I felt us suddenly lose altitude, and my stomach began to turn as Hal violently banked the aircraft to avoid the clouds and take us into a clearing.

"I told you this might happen, Rick!"

"But I thought we left with plenty of time to spare!"

"Weather's always unpredictable in Florida!"

Up ahead were more dark clouds. Hal took the yoke in one hand, the throttles in the other. I noticed his gold pinky ring that contained an engraved airplane propeller on it and another ring on his thumb finger. *This guy is too much!*

My heart was in my throat as we dove to the right and zig-zagged around the clouds. To the right. Then up and down.

"Can't you slow down?" I requested.

"And what? Allow these clouds to swallow us?"

He gunned the engines and smiled. *What the hell is that all about?* We were now banking to the left and then to the right.

I tried to crack a smile, but I tasted something I might have had for breakfast. I wouldn't be able to take any more of this. *If this were a car, I'd jump out and suffer the consequences.* The sharper the turn, the greater Hal's snicker.

"Hal, I'm having trouble dealing with your antics!"

"It's just another day when the skies are grey!" *What a clown! I should have ignored Mark's idea and insisted on driving.* Hal consistently maneuvered around, up, and down, avoiding the cloud formations for what seemed like an eternity.

Suddenly, I heard him bellow as he arched the aircraft into a dive to avoid a thundercloud.

He repeated, "Have no fear, Hal is here!" *Right . . . this ain't no amusement park ride!*

We finally leveled off, and Hal told me we had navigated through the worst of it. Thirty minutes into the flight, when I could breathe again, I stared at the airplane gauges as if I had been hypnotized. I must have been in a trance as the next thing I remember was the airplane bouncing on and off the ground at the Fort Lauderdale airport.

"I thought I'd give you a little something to remember me by," said Hal. "You've been a brave passenger and deserve a little good-bye bounce."

"Thanks a lot, Hal!" *This guy is deranged!*

"No problem. Just remember, 'When you need to fly, Hal's your guy!'"

"Okay!" *Enough with the rhyming!*

After we finished taxiing to the trailer, Hal cut the engines and I quickly opened the door and jumped onto the ground. Gathering my belongings, I bid him farewell and walked toward my car, which was parked behind the building. My head was spinning as I opened the trunk and placed the items in it.

I suddenly turned around, bent over, and dry-heaved behind the car. It was a good thing I hadn't eaten lunch.

Chapter 13

LONDONDERRY FAIRE

I arrived at the station one morning and heard a lively buzz emanating from the conference room.

"What's going on?" I asked salesperson Mike Malkin as I entered the room.

"Ken has been fired. He's cleaning out his office and moving back to Boston."

Wasting little time, I rushed into Ken's office. He was boxing up the last of his personal effects.

He turned to me and said, "Yes, it's true. I'm out of here."

"But, Ken," I replied, "you've been a major factor in my success here!"

"You'll be fine," he said. "It's time to spread your wings and put into practice what you've learned. In no time, you'll be managing. You've clearly got the stuff."

I paused for a moment to digest what he was saying. Ken had been the first manager to take any interest in my development. I felt as if I were losing my steadiest supporter.

"Well, if that's the case, thanks for everything, Ken. Will you be staying in the business?"

"Doubt it. I'm going to take some time to figure it all out."

"Makes sense," I said somewhat forlornly.

It was a bittersweet moment when he came around his desk and gave me a firm handshake.

"Take care," I continued. "Please give me a call when you get settled, okay?"

"Okay," he replied. "Now get your butt to the meeting!"

I turned and made my way to the conference room. When I arrived, I heard Mark Cole, WAXY's general manager, introducing the new sales manager, Steve Pierce. Steve had been the top biller at the time and the one with the most tenure, but he lacked management experience. The fact that he was a novice didn't thrill me. I also recognized his habit of spending a lot of his time at Fort Lauderdale bars. *I wonder if I can keep up with his after-hours drinking habit?*

Mark Cole headed one end of the conference table.

"Okay. Here's the big news! We have decided to stage a themed indoor festival in Coconut Grove the weekend before Thanksgiving to sell packages to retailers so that they can kick-start Christmas sales."

"How much time do we have to get the packages out and ready?" shouted out one of the sellers.

"I think Steve is working on the details, but we're looking at possibly six weeks."

"Six weeks!" I exclaimed. "How can we possibly sell and produce a program in that short time span?"

"You can do it!" remarked Steve with a sudden burst of confidence.

Perhaps we didn't have enough time to sell it, but the idea behind the event, Londonderry Faire, was a good one. Conceived by our corporate promotions maven, Ben Novack, the weekend event was to mimic an old London street complete with storefront facades, park benches, and those pathetic town criers, who would continually ring bells and announce useless information such as town happenings (in this case, promo messages for customers.) The "storefronts" were to be marketed to Miami area retailers to sell visitors Christmas gifts.

The station had committed to spending dollars to promote the event on television and in newspapers to ensure a large attendance.

Plans had already been made to hold the event at Dinner Key Auditorium, an aging waterfront airplane hangar in Coconut Grove that had been used by Pan American Airlines during its amphibious plane era. The auditorium had never been renovated and was showing its wear through rust-covered beams and broken windows. In addition, the hall wasn't air conditioned, which made for a potentially uncomfortable environment in the heat and humid air of South Florida, even in November.

"Now here's the deal," continued Mark. "I've asked Ben to come to town to introduce our next great promotional idea, haaaah, haaaah!"

Most of us knew Ben as the guy that ordered t-shirts and bumper stickers, but a major promotion?

"Now listen up!" continued Mark. "Several other stations in our company have already been out selling the concept and kicking butt! *You mean getting their butt kicked?* I'm going to let Ben take over and tell you about it."

Ben stood and handed out three colored sheets of paper to every salesperson. The details were spelled out in bits and pieces but lacked any cohesion. *So this is the fancy sales presentation, Ben? I've seen overnight commercial packages that looked more enticing!*

Ben went on to tell us how we were going to make large commissions from the sale of storefronts at Londonderry Faire. As an example, our sister station in Boston had just finished its event and garnered over $120,000 in retail sales, the top seller taking home a $10,000 commission check.

"This could be your ticket to a huge month," offered Ben. "When you think of all the exposure your customer will be receiving—storefront at the event, on-air promotional announcements, additional traffic—it's a no-brainer!"

When he finished his presentation, there were plenty of rolling eyes in the room. The sales team—a cynical bunch—quickly realized his hype didn't measure up to the quality of the promotion. I learned that if you couldn't sell the sales team on an idea, the likelihood of its success might be a stretch. *What does he take us for? Morons?*

Obviously, the six-week turnaround was a huge challenge, and the event was going to be exhausting: all day Saturday and Sunday in the heat, especially when Ben told us about the authentic turn-of-the-century costumes we'd be wearing.

As our interest in selling Londonderry Faire was poor from the start, and because we neglected to prospect enough businesses to make the event a sales success, it showed in our final results. Only twelve advertisers signed up, including an electronics retailer, a movie that was scheduled for Christmas release, a music store, a fresh-produce retailer, a florist and a gift/card store.

As we approached the deadline for maximum customer promotional benefit, only Mark and Steve maintained their enthusiasm.

"C'mon, guys," said Steve Pierce at a special sales meeting to psych us up. "Let's regroup and make a list of prospects you are going to close this week." The room was eerily silent. Finally, Mike Sparks spoke up: "I've got Banana Boat tanning products from Tahiti Beach." A chuckle filled the room as it was well-known that Mike had spent his free time on Tahiti's nude beach. It was equally well-known that on one fateful afternoon, he had taken off work early and gone for a swim in the ocean. When he returned to his blanket, all of his clothes were gone! *I could envision Mike huffing and puffing around the beach looking for something to wear home and explain*

to his unsuspecting wife what had happened! What a goofball.
"Who else?" beckoned Steve.

A list of advertisers—potential sponsors—were shouted out by our team: Luria's, Special Nails and Lashes, Hollywood Subaru, STP, Ziggy Boutique, Burdines. Of course we were telling Steve what he wanted to hear since many of the prospects had already said no to the idea.

"We're going to have to close these sponsors by Friday to identify them on all of our promotional announcements and print signs," continued Steve.

Several salesmen laughed.

"What's that about?" inquired Steve. *Oh . . . so now the laid-back former salesperson—now sales manager—has suddenly become a hard-ass!*

"Today's Monday, and that gives us just five days!" said Gene Lawson.

"I don't care," countered Steve. "Just do your best." *Now that's a really motivating management gem.*

The meeting broke up, and we returned to the sales pit to start making phone calls. Our efforts were mostly futile, and only one new advertiser signed up. In a last-ditch attempt to fill the auditorium, Steve opted to give away a few storefronts to existing advertisers, such as his "pet account," Women's Answers Abortion Clinic a Miami abortion center. *What could be a better match for an old English town than an abortion clinic?*

In addition, one of WAXY's sellers convinced Steve that he was working on a large, new advertiser and lobbied for some spare space to entice a station commitment. Steve agreed but, as it turned out, the advertiser was his mother who wanted to clean out her garage to sell her crap in one of the storefronts.

Coconut Grove was a 45-minute drive from Fort Lauderdale, and Mark Cole thought it would be best to acquire rooms for his attending staff members at the Marriott Airport Hotel, saving us the wear and tear of the commute.

"Think of it as a weekend adventure," Mark said as he handed out our hotel room keys.

"You bet," said Steve, who was smacking his lips at the thought of drinking vodka.

The town backdrop and props were scheduled to arrive on Friday morning at 10:00 a.m. so our clients would have plenty of time to set up for Saturday and Sunday.

"We'll have them moved in by 1 p.m.," Mark assured us.

By 9:30 a.m., trucks containing our sponsors' items were lining up outside the auditorium. Unfortunately, by 11:30 a.m., the Londonderry Faire props hadn't arrived and our customers were starting to overheat and become grumpy. Several were outspoken about the now defunct move-in schedule. *This really sucks. Now what?*

"I've got a ton of electronics in my truck and two inventory guys I've plucked from our store," remarked Peter Poskin from ABC Stereo. "When are these street props going to arrive? And how long will I have to keep my guys away from the store?"

Other customers were gossiping among themselves. I overheard one venting.

"This isn't going to happen. I have a feeling that I've been ripped off," she said. "I'm ready to call the *Miami Herald* and make this disaster a news story." *Great. I can see the headlines now: "Radio Station Unfair to Customers About Coconut Grove Faire."*

We did our best to pacify our customers by buying lunch and cold beer in an effort to restore calm to the crowd and assure them that the props would arrive at any minute. We were wrong. By the time the trucks arrived at 3:00 p.m., many of the advertisers (especially the ones who refused to drink with us) demanded refunds. *Damn teetotalers!*

The construction of Londonderry Faire's storefronts and street lamps was completed by 7:00 p.m., and by 10:30 p.m. we had moved in all of our remaining sponsors. Our final sponsor count was nine. Undeterred by this setback, Mark offered to take us back to the hotel.

"C'mon," Steve beckoned to the sales force after conferring with Mark. "We're going to put this fiasco behind us and relax over a few drinks and dinner."

Drinks? Did I hear drinks?

No one in attendance disagreed. Following a quick road trip to the hotel and dressed in ragged perspiration-stained clothing, we ate dinner and drank away our frustration from the long day. We finally closed the bar at 2:00 a.m., many of us having learned a few lines of Spanish to speak with the waitress. *¿Puedo tener otra bebida, por favor?* (*Can I have another drink, please?*)

Since Londonderry Faire was scheduled to open its doors at 10:00 a.m., I struggled out of bed. After rocking in the shower from a giant-sized hangover, I was barely able to don my costume and drive to Dinner Key in time. *I hope I don't get stopped along the way by the police. They'd probably figure I'm mentally ill!*

When I arrived, I noticed Gene Lawson dressed in tights, a brass-buttoned long-tail coat, and a triangular hat.

"Nice outfit, Gene," I shouted.

"You, too," he said. "What character are you supposed to be?"

"Beats me. I just hope I don't see anyone I know!"

We were both laughing as more sellers arrived, all dressed in English turn-of-the-century costumes, which included the ever-present white tights. It didn't take long for the heat and humidity to take their toll, so wigs and hats were removed and cold beer was made available in the rear of an empty storefront. Only a few dozen attendees were waiting outside when the doors opened at 11:00 a.m., an ominous sign.

The event went from bad to worse, as only 200 visitors attended the two-day event. And those "shoppers" were mostly "lookers" and were as humored as we were.

"This was worth the price of admission just to see grown men in tights," I overheard one saying.

"What a joke! Who came up with this gem of an idea?" inquired another.

Our customers weren't as humored. In an effort to please them, we circulated around the auditorium to offer free commercial schedules. Some refused and demanded refunds.

To Mark Cole's dismay, nothing good came out of Londonderry Faire. Only six paying sponsors actually participated during the two-day event and the number of empty storefronts dwarfed those that were actually occupied.

As one spectator so comically put it, "From what I can see, the town of Londonderry should file Chapter XI."

In the end, we made the most of the weekend. My two advertisers were eventually thankful for the free beer and time away from their store. The abortion clinic's female manager invited several station employees upstairs to an empty office for an afternoon tryst. We survived a weekend wearing costumes from an era I won't soon forget.

And Mark's *haaaah, haaaah* could be heard echoing throughout Dinner Key's hollow confines all weekend. *Just another experience that will go down in the annals of a giant promotional failure!*

Chapter 14

MY CLIENT, THE JUDGE

In the late 1970s, Fort Lauderdale's nightlife was comprised of an arcade of drinking delights that included singles' drinking bars, discos, private clubs, and topless bars. Many of these advertised on WAXY, several of which I handled personally.

There were times that I worked with clubs that weren't advertisers if it would benefit a prospective client or fill a need for a station contest. The idea was to make a good impression with the prospect so he'd buy a schedule. Jeremy Scott, one of my contacts in the public relations business, brought me such a promotional opportunity.

Jeremy worked with a trendy Fort Lauderdale singles' bar, The Rose. I had often approached Jeremy with sales packages but was unable to sell him. His priority (and the reason he had been retained by the client) was to orchestrate free promotions with stations that would involve a variety of unique "singles' nights" to continually attract good-looking girls and, naturally, the men who followed them. His successful promotions brought in large crowds and profits for the club and kept his client happy.

Jeremy contacted me with an invitation to participate in an upcoming promotion at The Rose, where patrons were fond of generously poured cocktails. The bar's décor was a tropical island theme complete with tacky plastic palm trees and a giant bamboo hut that extended over the large bar.

"Rick, it's Jeremy Scott. How are you?" he asked.

"Hi, Jeremy. How's the club business? Still working them?"

"Of course, Rick. Gotta go where the money is! In fact, I'm putting together a promotion for The Rose for next Thursday and thought of you because I need a judge for our "Lady T-shirt" contest. Don't you work with Crown David, the dude who frequently appears on television? His commercials are some of the corniest I've ever seen. Everyone knows Crown David, and he'd make a great judge for our contest. What do you think?"

"'Lady T-shirt' contest? Isn't that a bit over the edge for even a guy like David?" I asked.

"Nah. He'll love the attention and the idea of meeting some good-looking girls. This isn't a wet T-shirt contest, Rick. It's being held at a classy club." *What planet are you from? The place is filled with customers who wear T-shirts and cutoffs!*

Thinking it might be a bit of a stretch, but rationalizing that David's ego was involved, I caved. "Let me contact him, Jeremy. It's last minute, and he's a busy guy."

"Tell you what, Rick. Let him know I'll even buy dinner at The Fork, the four-star restaurant adjacent to the club."

"Free dinner? You do know that he's a big fan of fancy dining. It might just clinch the deal. I'll give him a call and get back to you later today."

"Thanks, Rick. It should be a night he won't forget!"

I knew better than to ever work on a nightclub promotion without selling a schedule but reasoned it would further cement my connection with Crown David. A likeable guy in his early forties, David had made his fortune in the automotive business. I picked up the phone and dialed his direct line.

"Hello. David here," he answered.

"Hi, David. It's Rick Charnack at WAXY."

"Oh, yes, Rick. How are you doing? I've got a check here with WAXY's name on it for last month's schedule."

"Great," I replied," but that's not why I'm calling."

"Okay."

"I know how much you enjoy being in the public eye, and I think I've got something right down your alley. You're familiar with The Rose, right?"

"Sure. Who isn't? Been there once or twice for a drink, and it always seems to attract a good-looking crowd. Love those ladies!"

"Well, a friend of mine who owns a public relations firm thought you'd make a great judge for next Thursday's "Lady T-shirt" promotion. You know—the one where the girl with the sexiest T-shirt dress wins a prize! He's offered to buy dinner for us before the contest next door at The Fork. What do you say?"

"You're kidding me, right?" He wants to buy us dinner at The Fork and have me judge a room full of ladies?"

"That's right."

"Hmmm . . . twist my arm, Rick. What time?"

"We'll meet for dinner at 8 p.m., and the promotion starts at nine-thirty."

"Next Thursday, right? Sure. I can be there at eight!"

"Great. I'll see you there. You want me to continue to run your same commercial schedule this month?"

"Okay. And I'll bring the check with me on Thursday."

"Sounds like a deal. Thanks, David. See you then."

I hung up the phone and realized that I had just killed three birds with one stone. First, I had confirmed an order for more commercials from David; second, I had secured an ego-stroking event for him as a judge at a rather risqué event;

and third, had arranged for my client to bring a check for his latest schedule.

I phoned Jeremy with the good news.

"It's a deal," I said. "You can count on David to judge next week's contest."

"Excellent," replied Jeremy. "I'll set your dinner reservations for eight and come around nine so we can review the details."

"Terrific. See you then."

During the week leading up to the promotion, I had second thoughts about involving one of my good clients, especially one as upstanding as Crown David, in a potentially sullied event. Until now, David's reputation had been built on his business integrity and clever television and radio advertising. He was a cute man with round cheeks and a bit of a belly that prevented his tie from dropping below his belt—other than that, he dressed the way you'd expect from an auto dealer: sport coat (of the polyester variety), matching slacks, tie, and an ever-present tie clasp. His larger-than-life persona made him the consummate master of ceremonies.

Meeting him inside The Fork did little to allay my fears. There he was, conspicuously waiting for me at a corner table wearing his trademark sport coat, shirt, and tie replete with clasp. I was impressed with his nobility. Taking a seat across the table from him, I opened the conversation with a compliment.

"You look great, David," I said. "Always ready for the camera!" *Oh my God, what did I just say? This is not a promotion where he should be on any camera!*

"Looking good yourself, Rick," he replied. "Did you come directly from work?"

I hadn't had a chance to go home, clean up, and put on a fresh shirt. "I don't know where the time goes these days!"

"I know you're a hard worker. Perhaps we might talk sometime about you coming to work with me." *I don't think so. No polyester in my future!*

"Thanks, David. I think I'm set for now. Let's order dinner. I'm starved."

"Me, too."

I signaled the waiter to our table. David had already been sipping on a scotch so I ordered another round and asked if he was ready to order. He nodded and looked at the menu.

"Bring me a half-dozen oysters, wedge salad, lamb chops (three double chops with rosemary au jus), macaroni and cheese and creamed spinach. Oh, and another side order of asparagus. And, before I forget, get the chocolate soufflé ready for dessert." *What's this—your last meal?*

My order was modest: mixed greens salad, dry-aged sirloin, and baked potato.

"Would you like wine with your dinner?" asked the waiter.

"Not unless you want some," I said, looking at David.

"I'm fine with my scotch."

"I'm fine as well."

David turned to me to find out more about the promotion. I directed his attention to a sign at the hallway connecting The Fork and The Rose. The sign included his name and the upcoming event:

"Join *Crown David* and the sexiest girls in town at *The Rose's* Thursday SEXY DRESS CONTEST. Wear your hottest T-shirt dress and win $500. Contest starts at 9:30 p.m.! See you there!"

Proud as a newborn dad, David stood up in his chair and remarked, "Not too bad. In fact, I like it!" *Sure you do. It's your friggin' name there!*

Jeremy arrived promptly at 9:00 p.m., sat down at our table, and ordered a beer. After I made the introduction, Jeremy turned to David.

"You ready?" he asked.

"Absolutely!"

"Here's how it will work. I've set up a stage where there's room for you and a "contestant" to stand so that you'll be in full view of the patrons. Shortly before 10:00 p.m. you'll begin calling out for contestants on the microphone and, one by one, invite them to join you on the stage. You'll ask the crowd to vote and, based on their applause, I'll record the results. We'll continue to do this until 11:30 p.m., at which time you'll announce the winner. Got it?"

"Yes," said David. "You'll keep score, right?"

"That's right. One more thing," said Jeremy. "These events can get out of hand sometimes, so be careful not to incite the crowd too much."

"What do you mean?"

"Well, last time a contestant took off her shirt and a customer started sipping Grand Marnier from her chest." *What have I done? I could actually LOSE his account!*

"I'll do my best to stay cool." *Sure you will.*

By the time we finished dinner, it was almost 9:45 p.m. It appeared that David was feeling no pain after ingesting two scotches. Jeremy escorted us through a brief connecting hallway to The Rose's bar, which was filled wall to wall with customers. The crowd immediately recognized David, and a cheer went out for him. He was led to the stage area where Jeremy handed him a microphone.

"Hi, everyone!" said David. "I'm certain we're all here for the same thing. And that "thing" will be me putting $500 into the sexiest t-shirt dress-wearing hottie!" *You mean "in the underwear of the sexiest t-shirt hottie." Want another scotch?*

Someone yelled, "Let's get the show on the road!"

David replied, "Okay. Who's going to be first?"

An overweight woman with dyed blonde hair and drooping breasts stepped up onto the stage. Her T-shirt hung all the way to her knees. "Boo!" yelled several men in the crowd.

"Let's get on with it!" shouted a mustached man in a vested suit.

"Okay," said David, "who's next?"

A few minutes went by and the next contestant appeared, wearing a yacht captain's hat on top of what appeared to be bleached blonde hair, a tight-fitting long T-shirt with "Tits Ahoy" emblazed on it, and no bra but breasts standing at attention. It appeared as if she had taken the night off from a local strip club with her own cheering section.

"Okay, audience. What do you think?"

The crowd shouted out their approval and Jeremy, close at hand, was more than willing to help contestant number two down from the stage, afterward making a notation on his clipboard. I overheard David making a comment to Jeremy, like "Wow, how are we going to top this?"

Meanwhile, the barmaids had wide smiles on their faces as it was a night where tips were plentiful. The overflow crowd required their constant attention and they were pouring drinks dreaming of what they might buy with the huge "take" from the evening. "I'm Your Boogie Man" by KC and the Sunshine Band blared from overhead speakers.

The next contestant stepped up to a thunderous round of applause. She was intoxicated and had long brown hair that extended to her waist, a bust line that almost knocked Crown David off the stage, and a T-shirt that flowed just short of her derrière. He could barely speak above the catcalls and screams, taking his time to closely examine her wares.

"Ah . . . how. . . er . . . what do you think?" David stuttered, trying to speak through the microphone and gauge the audience's response to her.

The crowd erupted with thunderous whistles and catcalls.

"More, more, more, more!" they yelled in unison.

And so for the next hour or so, beauties and not-so-beauties stood in line for their chance to win the prize. David was in a "zone," helping contestants up to the stage for their shot at $500. Unfortunately, there were many who shouldn't have been there, and several Jeremy invited as "ringers" from his strip club client, Juicy Fruit. All was going well until several Juicy Fruit girls became entrepreneurial, flashing their breasts for tips and allowing patrons to stuff dollar bills in their underwear. In the midst of all of the emotional upheaval, one of the barmaids ran over to me.

"A neighbor from next door who's obsessed with stopping our promotion sent a spy over and has complained about the scantily dressed ladies," she said. "I think she's called the police! You better get Crown David out of here unless you want him to get busted!"

"Thanks," I said. "You've done me a big favor." I took out a $10 bill from my wallet and gave it to her.

"Thank you!" she winked. "Come by anytime, and I'll buy you a drink!"

I began to push my way through the crowd to the stage to tell David that he was in potential danger. He was so engrossed in the promotion that he waved me off.

"But they're going to arrest you!" I yelled.

"What?" he replied.

"I said this place is about to be busted!" At this point, I was almost screaming at him.

"Then let's get the hell out of here!"

David stepped down from the stage, leaving alone a statuesque beauty who grabbed the back of his sport coat, attempting to pull him back on stage. It failed. I began pushing people out of my way. The crowd was shouting, "David! David! David!"

Finally, we reached The Rose's back door.

"Where are *you* going?" asked a customer who appeared to have had far too much to drink. "Get Crown David back on stage!"

"I'm going out that door," I insisted. "And I suggest that you do the same!"

"No, you aren't!"

David, who was now moving quickly, reached around me and pushed the patron out of the way.

"Screw you!" remarked David. "Yes, we are."

I was shocked by David's spontaneous outburst but appreciated the move. We both headed out the door and to his car in the rear of the building.

"Take it easy, David. Make certain you drive straight home."

"Not to worry. I understand."

As David drove off, I heard sirens in the distance. I ran to my car. Headlights off, I drove through the alley in back of The Rose onto a side street.

My nerves were shot from what I had just witnessed. I needed a drink and decided to drive the short distance to Up-Town, a popular Fort Lauderdale dance club. When I arrived, I noticed the parking lot jammed full of cars but managed to fit in a tiny space near the road.

"Double scotch," I said as I pulled up a chair at the bar.

The place was filled with a more upscale crowd, most of whom were dressed to kill—girls in dresses that left nothing to the imagination and men in vested suits, not in T-shirts like at The Rose. "Fly, Robin, Fly" swelled the giant speakers throughout the disco. It was a refreshing change from the insanity of The Rose.

I did a quick go-round of the bar, looking for single girls, and noticed mostly coupled-off patrons. I checked the dance floor. Same. I quickly finished my drink, and as I made my way out the door to walk to my car, I heard someone scream.

"It's YOU!" hollered a former contestant who recognized me from The Rose. From her looks, I gathered that she was one of the Juicy Fruit girls.

"They busted The Rose a few minutes ago and have charged the manager and promotions guy with lewd and lascivious activity at the bar," she said, slurring her words. "They are looking for Crown David and, if I were you, I'd make certain he's not around. And to top it off, I just saw a car crash in the parking lot!"

I recalled that Crown David's name was in large letters on the promotional poster and had we not been tipped off by the barmaid, both of us might had been arrested. The contestant continued to rant and rave about how she should have won.

"It's your fault," she said, as if she'd already spent the $500.

"My fault?" I said. "I didn't call the police. It was the girls who showed their tits to the crowd that got the place busted. Weren't you one of them?"

"Of course," she said. "We do it all the time. The Juicy Fruit girls always win the contests. Didn't you hear us screaming for each other? Want to make it up to me? Come inside and buy me a drink."

I thought about it for a second but guessed she was still "working." *Forget it, Rick. It's t-r-o-u-b-l-e with a capital T!*

"Sorry, I can't right now but I'll see you at Juicy Fruit. What's your name?"

"Cinnamon. But you can call me 'Buns'! All of my customers know what I'm famous for!"

"Okay, Buns. I'll check you out sometime."

"Have it your way," she huffed and hurriedly walked through the door, almost tripping on the entrance landing.

I walked through the jammed parking lot toward my car.

As I approached it, I stopped in disbelief. The driver's side of my car had been sideswiped by another vehicle. A large crease on the front fender was visible, as well as paint chips hanging from the door. The front bumper was pushed forward and away from the wheel-well. Ironically, it was *my car* that she described as having just been in a crash.

Thankfully, the damage wasn't enough to prevent me from driving home. Embarrassed as I was from motoring with a rearranged fender, I was able to make it without incident. By the time I got home, it was after 3:00 a.m.

The following morning, I awoke to visions of my client being arrested, handcuffed, and taken away by the Fort Lauderdale police. I quickly showered, dressed, and sped off to Crown David's place of business. His office door was open, so I walked in and slid into a comfortable chair, prepared to discuss what I had heard and to take the blame for all of the troubles from the night before. I began explaining the danger he was in but instead he cut me off.

"I received a call this morning from my close friend Sergeant Harris at the Fort Lauderdale Police Department. He told me that he'd heard that I was at a bar hosting a lewd show last night."

"Aha," I said, anxiously waiting for him to tell me the rest of the story.

"You want to know what he told me?"

"Sure. I think so."

"He told me that next time I host an event like that, I'd better invite him. Seems as if he knows several of the Juicy Fruit girls first hand, that horny rabbit!"

"Really?" I said as we both chuckled.

"Perhaps we might arrange to do another promotion at their club?" *Are you kidding? Not on your life!*

It was time to leave. *Always best to leave on a high note.* I got up, shook David's hand, and walked to the door of his office. Reaching the door, I said, "It was a good time, right?"

"Absolutely," he responded. "And I'd do it again in a heartbeat!"

Chapter 15

ARE WE GOING TO SAN FRANCISCO?

It was late on Friday, a time of the week when most of the WAXY staff would typically unwind at a bar fronting the Intracoastal Waterway in Fort Lauderdale. On this particular Friday, the staff was more than willing to gather because it was the birthday of my sales manager, Bobby O'Brien. Bobby had been appointed local sales manager when Steve Pierce transferred to a popular station owned by the same company in San Francisco.

Linda Martini, the sales secretary, chose Bootleggers mostly because we had barter credit with the restaurant. The station had provided advertisements in exchange for food and beverages.

"Bootleggers it is," I said, looking forward to ending the week on a literal high.

"See you there," replied Linda, as those sellers who remained in the sales office began their mass exodus.

"Did you buy a cake?" I whispered to Linda.

"Forget the cake, Rick. By the time we leave Bootleggers, Bobby won't even know what day it is!"

The drive to the restaurant took less than ten minutes and, upon arrival, our party of nine gravitated to the table nearest the water. The group included four sellers; WAXY's receptionist Donna Luther; the general manager's secretary, Pam Wise; Linda; and Bobby.

Linda and Donna were sisters from Maryland and extremely attractive. Linda had brilliant blonde hair worn down over her shoulders, facial features that included the high cheekbones common in Southern belles, and typically dressed in high-class fashion with crepe blouses and colorful scarfs. She drove a hot yellow sports car. Donna, the younger of the two, was my favorite. She was more earthy looking and wore jeans and tight-fitting tops that showed off her enormous breasts, which she used to tease any or every man with whom she came in contact. It had been rumored that she and the station engineer were having an affair.

As the "birthday boy," Bobby was directed to the head of the table. He was approaching his sixties, Irish (always chose a green car), and short in stature so that the chair seemed to swallow him. The waitress took our drink order. It was a warm, breezy night in Fort Lauderdale, and Bobby appeared relaxed.

"It's a great night to have a birthday," said Bobby, peering at the boats cruising down the waterway.

"It will be an even better night as soon as the drinks arrive," offered salesperson Gene Lawson, who was sitting next to Bobby. Gene was a well-dressed seller on the team, illustrated by his crisp dress shirts and the excellence with which his ties were knotted. He always had a Wild Turkey in his hand and often led pub crawls with WAXY salespersons.

A few minutes later, the waitress appeared with a tray full of cocktails that included an extra-large cocktail glass, the size of which one might mistake for a small Jacuzzi.

"This one's for you," she cackled. "Happy birthday, Bobby!"

"I can't drink that much scotch," he replied.

"C'mon," she answered. "Live it up. It's your birthday!" As soon as we all had our drinks in hand, Gene stood up and asked us to raise our glasses.

"Here's to our fearless leader. A true Irishman who loves his scotch! Happy Birthday, Bobby!"

In unison, those at the table stood up and shouted, "Happy Birthday, Bobby!" Our shouts brought critical stares from other bar patrons. Linda, who was sitting next to me, leaned over and said, "Screw them, RC. They just don't know how to have fun."

Another one of the sellers, Ron Barclay, stood up and gave another toast.

"Mr. Carson, may this night set your head right!" *Oh, no, this can't be good. Ron's already got a buzz on!*

Ron was the most brazen seller at WAXY. His sense of humor and outlandish pranks and stunts were only second to his admiration for beautiful women. A tall, moustached, good-looking man in his thirties, he might be considered one of Fort Lauderdale's most eligible bachelors if not for his status as a married man.

On one occasion, his best friend on the sales team, Rob Carston, was politicking for the job of sales manager after Steve Pierce had transferred to our company's station in San Francisco (the position for which Bobby was eventually hired). When he didn't get the job, Ron arranged to have Rob rolled into the office in a casket, perfectly dressed in a suit and tie and with white powder on his face to simulate a funeral home viewing.

"Here lies Rob Carston, who died from disappointment over not being appointed sales manager at WAXY Radio," said Ron while presiding over the service and the open casket. A dozen WAXY staffers had gathered and stood gazing into the casket in disbelief. Several were laughing hysterically.

Hearing the commotion from his office, the station's general manager, Norm Beeman appeared within view of the casket. Norm had worked in CBS's corporate environment prior to coming to WAXY and had little tolerance for frivolity.

"What's going on here?" he demanded.

"Rob Carston has passed on," replied Ron. A spontaneous burst of laughter filled the room.

"Get him out!" commanded Norm.

"Not before we pray," said Ron.

"No, right now!" Norm crabbed. "And report to my office after you return the casket and Rob washes his face." *Uh oh, he's gone too far now.*

After closing the casket with Rob in it, several of us followed Ron as he rolled it out of the radio station door and then through the front door of the building. There was a waiting hearse double-parked on the street. Gene Lawson was among us.

"You better get back here as soon as you can," chirped Gene. "Norm's really pissed!"

"No worry," Rob responded, as he stepped out of the casket. "Not before Ron and I have a liquid lunch." *Great idea! Maybe I'll join them.*

I returned to the office where staff members were still milling about with wide grins. There was a buzz in the air. As I sat down at my desk, Gene walked over to me. "You better find Ron and tell them both to get back here now! They're in big trouble, and getting drunk will get them fired for sure."

"Okay," I told him, "but you owe me." *Now this prank could also get me fired!*

I grabbed my car keys and exited through the station back door. I drove up Federal Highway to the funeral home where Ron had befriended the owner. Sure enough, there was the hearse, parked in front of the entrance blocking traffic. I doubled parked on the street in front of it and ran into the building. There they were, Rob with his powdered suit and Ron laughing.

"Ron!" I called out.

"R.C.," he shouted back.

I quickly walked up to him.

"Gene told me to come and get you guys. You need to get back to the station ASAP if you want your jobs. You know Norm's sense of humor is nonexistent."

"Okay. We're on our way."

Later in the afternoon, Ron returned and somehow managed to keep his job, telling Norm that he had gotten caught up in the emotion of the prank and regretted his involvement. He was scolded and sent back to his desk. When he returned to the sales bullpen, he and Gene let out a roaring laugh.

However, that was the last I saw of Rob Carston. He never came back to the station as the disappointment of losing a promotion was just too much. It was rumored that he was appointed sales manager at a radio station in Philadelphia, a much larger radio market, and fitting irony to his career disappointment in Fort Lauderdale.

On this particular night, Ron made his toast and refused to sit down. He called over our waitress and put his arm around her. Directing his attention to me, he spoke.

"Look at the pretty girl, R.C.! Doesn't she have great cheekbones?" *I can't imagine how embarrassing this must be for her! I feel for you, honey.*

"Oh, sit down, Ron," shouted Bobby.

"Yes, sir, birthday boy," saluted Ron.

And so it went for the next several hours. Drinks were brought to the table, and Gene and Bobby amused us with stories of their career in radio advertising. Bobby's large glass of scotch was refilled numerous times, and he began to giggle like a school kid.

"I'm as high as a kite," he commented at one point. Most of us were feeling the same way. Gary and Ron began to dare each other to entertain us with their funny pranks. Ron continued to embarrass "pretty girls" by bringing them over to the table. Gary challenged us to drink a shot of tequila with him, and nobody protested.

"R.C., it's your turn," said Gene. I nodded my head and scanned the table. Directly in front of me was a condiment holder with salt and pepper and sugar packets. I lifted it off the table, tossed it into the water, and watched as it disappeared from view. A round of applause let out from the table.

"Now for the big one," shouted Bobby. "You don't have a hair on your head unless you take Donna and Pam to visit Steve Pierce in San Francisco tonight!" *Is he kidding? He obviously doesn't know who he's dealing with!*

"You ladies up for it?" I asked.

"Sure," responded Pam.

"Let's go! Get over to the phone booth and make reservations NOW!" said Donna.

"You're paying for it, Bobby?" I asked.

"Sure," he replied, taking a long sip of his scotch. "Just trust me!"

I stood up and walked through the overflowing Friday night crowd to the phone booth and noticed a tall blonde on the phone. She was apparently arguing with someone whom I guessed was her boyfriend.

"I'm going to really get drunk now," I overheard her saying. "Why don't you go screw yourself!" I watched as she slammed down the receiver. She gathered her handbag, slid the door open, and said, "It's all yours!" I slid by her into the

booth—her lingering perfume smacking me in the face—
placed a quarter into the pay slot, and dialed 411.

"Delta Airlines," I said to the directory assistance opera-
tor.

"Here's the number," she replied. "Would you like me to
dial it for you? Recognizing my now impaired faculties, I told
her, "Sure."

Roughly fifteen minutes later, I emerged from the booth
and headed over to our table.

"There's a flight that leaves at ten-fifteen. It's now nine-
thirty, which gives us about a half-hour to get our butts to
the airport!"

"We're out of here," said Bobby, signaling for the check.
The waitress sensed that we were in a hurry and responded
by handing the check to Bobby. He signed it, took out cash
for the tip, and we hurried off to our cars.

"I'll take the lead, so follow me," offered Bobby.

"Leave your car here, R.C.," said Gene. "You can take a cab
from the airport when you come back." Linda, Donna, and
Pam joined me in Gene's car, and we sped off following
Bobby.

"This guy's drunk," I overheard Linda saying to Gene.

"We're all drunk!" I told her.

"Pray that we get to the airport in one piece," offered Pam.

We followed Bobby as he sped through the streets of Fort
Lauderdale but slowed down when we hit a traffic jam on U.S.
1. It was a busy Friday night, and the cars were backed up at
the Sunrise Boulevard traffic light. We saw him leaning out of
his window, apparently yelling at the driver in front of him
while blaring his horn.

"Let's go! Get out of my way!"

The driver didn't appreciate Bobby's rudeness, opened his
door, and yelled something back. Again, Bobby leaned on his

horn, shouting obscenities to the driver. In a flash, the driver opened his door and got out. He was short—about five feet, three inches—had a slight build, and was yelling something at Bobby. The traffic light turned green, and cars were now passing us. Bobby opened his door and stepped forward to the creep who was now holding us up. I looked at my watch—9:55 p.m., so only five minutes to get to the airport!

Suddenly, I saw Bobby pounce on the driver, striking him in his head. The driver fell to the ground. *Okay, let's pretend this didn't happen.* *"Drunk Driver Slams Pedestrian to the Ground" was a headline I imagined in the morning newspaper.*

"Now get the hell up and drive!" demanded Bobby.

"Okay, okay," replied the driver. Bobby retreated to his car, crimson color on his cheekbones.

"Follow me!" he shouted to us.

I closed my eyes and was trying to block my senses from what felt like screeching stops and quick starts. At one point, I think we drove on the curb to pass several slow vehicles. *Thank God I'm inebriated!* We turned off U.S. 1 at the airport exit. Bobby continued to drive like a madman until both cars pulled up to Delta Airlines curb. It was 10:05 p.m. I took Donna and Pam by the hand and jumped out of the car. Bobby and Gene were standing by the cars laughing like hyenas.

"Enjoy the trip!" yelled Bobby.

"Watch out for those two, R.C.! They may bite!" teased Gene. *I hope so.*

"Happy Birthday, Bobby," I said. "Thanks for the treat!"

The three of us ran quickly toward the Delta ticket counter and in front of several waiting passengers.

"Our plane leaves in ten minutes," crowed Donna. The ticket agent heard her and began the ticketing process.

"Any bags?" he asked.

"None," I replied.

"All the way to San Francisco with no baggage?"

"Just finish the tickets so we can get out of here!" screamed a nervous Pam. *Oh, great. Now we're getting the fifth degree from a ticket agent and Pam's acting out. Just the kind of passengers they want on their plane!*

The agent completed the process, handing us our tickets, and we ran off to the gate. When we arrived, the gate area was empty, but the door was still open. *Oh crap! Did they pull the airplane back?* We showed our tickets to the agent and scurried down the jetway to the waiting aircraft. A flight attendant greeted us as we boarded.

"We were about to close the door," she exclaimed. "Take your seats immediately!"

I held Donna's hand as we walked the length of the airplane to row 38, the next-to-last row. Practically falling into our seats from exhaustion, we fastened our seat belts. *Am I really doing this? Is it the alcohol, or am I excited to be with two beautiful girls?* The flight attendant announced that we were on flight 433, service to Atlanta and then on to San Francisco. Pam turned to me with an annoying look.

"We've got to go to Atlanta first?" she griped.

"Yes," I replied, "but I'm certain it will be a fast stop."

"I'm looking at the schedule here," cried Donna, leafing through the booklet of flight times she had retrieved from the seat pocket. "We don't arrive in San Francisco until two a.m.!"

"Okay, settle down. We'll have plenty of time to relax, have a few drinks, see a movie on board. Let's take one step at a time."

"Great idea, Rick," said Donna, holding onto my arm. "Let's have a drink."

Pam broke in, interrupting that thought. "You're not going to believe what movie they're showing! It's *Blazing Saddles!*"

"That's great," I echoed. "We'll be laughing our assess off all the way to San Francisco."

"With a few drinks in us, anything's possible," smiled Donna. *I'm going nuts in here. Is she really coming on to me on board this jet?*

The flight to Atlanta landed on time. We knocked down two drinks each, and once the plane emptied, we spread out, ready for a nap. Because of the time of day of the flight, the boarding passengers took less than half of the seats. I checked on Pam and Donna and noticed that they were both fast asleep. I put my head down on my pillow, and the next thing I felt was Donna's hand shaking me.

"They're getting ready to start the movie. I'm thirsty, so let's order a drink." *A drink? That's the last thing I'm thinking about ordering.*

"Sure, Donna." I pressed the overhead button, and a flight attendant appeared. We ordered, and Donna opened a blanket that covered the both of us. I felt her hand on my thigh. Suddenly Pam appeared in our row. "Got room for me?" she asked. Donna quickly removed her hand and placed it on top of the blanket.

"Sure," responded Donna. "Why don't you move over next to us?"

I looked at Donna, who was rolling her eyes, obviously disappointed by Pam's sudden interruption.

The drinks continued to flow during the five-hour flight to San Francisco. At one point, a flight attendant had to calm us down because we were laughing so loud during the movie.

"I don't remember a time when I drank so much," I boasted to the girls. "I'm surprised that I haven't passed out by now."

"R.C., you can handle it," replied Donna. "The best thing to do is keep on drinking!" *She's out of control. What's next? Pocket pool with a body part under the blanket?*

I turned my attention to the movie. Thankfully, by the time it ended, we were only an hour away from San Francisco. We finally disembarked to a deserted terminal—weary, jet-lagged, and ready for bed. "I think my boss has a corporate account at all Hilton Hotels," said Pam. "I've got one of his business cards, so let's use it!"

We walked through the terminal and exited onto the arrival curb. I felt a sudden chill run up my spine as the temperature was at least 30 degrees cooler than South Florida. We ran over to a taxi, jumped in, and cuddled inside.

"Hilton Hotel," I said, shivering. The cab drove away.

"Is it always this cold here?" I questioned the cab driver. "Yes, especially if you are planning to stay downtown. Lately it tops out at forty-five." *Forty-five? Just the thought brings visions of bronchitis.*

We arrived safely at the Hilton. I paid the driver, and we walked into the lobby and up to the reception desk of the Hilton. It was 2:45 a.m.

"Yes, I'd like a room for one night," declared Pam. "Please charge the room to Norm Beeman at WAXY Radio."

"Okay, let's see," replied the agent. After a few minutes fumbling with a keyboard, he looked at Pam. "I'm sorry, we don't have WAXY or Norm Beeman in our database."

"But there must be a mistake. I've made reservations for him at Hilton Hotels before, always on his corporate account."

"Is there any other name attached to the account?"

"Well, try Metro Radio." The agent fumbled some more and said, "I found it. But I need his credit card number."

"Credit card number? I don't have his credit card with me."

"Why don't you call him?" offered Donna, slurring her words.

"I can't call him. It's three in the morning!"

"Closer to six, Fort Lauderdale time," I explained.

"Okay, may I use your phone?" Pam inquired.

The agent handed her a desk phone while Pam looked through her handbag, leafing through a small red address book for Norm's number.

"Here it is," she said, triumphantly.

"Okay, make it a quick call," I responded. "Tell Norm you decided to visit a friend in San Francisco and you need to check in at the Hilton for one night." Pam dialed the phone, and I noticed her hand was shaking. After what appeared to be numerous rings, she spoke up.

"Norm, did I wake you? Sorry, but I'm in a jam and need your help. Last night at Bobby's birthday party at Bootlegger's, I made an impulsive decision to fly to San Francisco to visit a friend for the weekend. . . . What? . . . That's right, I know, it was entirely impulsive. . . . Who else? Just Rick and Donna . . . Yes, they acted on impulse, too. It was a crazy party. I'm sorry to call so early, but we need a place to crash, and since I always book you at Hilton Hotels I thought I could check in here. Can you help us? . . . Right, it's just one night, and then we'll stay at my friend's tomorrow. . . . Yes, he's right here."

Pam handed the phone to the agent, and he began writing down some information.

"Okay, sir," he said. "Just one night." He handed the phone back to Pam.

"Uh-huh. But Norm," pleaded Pam. "Okay, we'll talk on Monday." *She's in a world of hurt now. Wait until he finds out that Bobby will be submitting it as a station sales expense!!*

Pam handed the receiver to the desk agent. He asked for her credit card to cover any additional expenses. While she was signing the registration card, he handed me a room key.

"Thanks," Pam told the agent.

Opening the door to our room, I watched as both Pam and

Donna ran past. They jumped on one of the double beds and asked me to turn off the light. It was obvious that the seven-hour drunk-fest had done us all in. They quickly fell asleep with their clothes on. I took a quick shower and fully expected Donna to meet me; however, when I returned to the bedroom, I found both girls still fast asleep. I put my head on a pillow and took a deep breath. *What a crazy night! Who would have believed it? All of this over a dare?*

I awoke suddenly to a room fully lit from the large windows. Pam and Donna were talking about going somewhere. I looked at the clock radio. It was 9:15 a.m.

"Good morning," I said, my throat burning like a barbeque grill.

"Welcome back to the land of the living," replied Donna.

"What have you girls got up your sleeve this morning?"

"Well, a large breakfast would be great for starters," offered Pam.

"I agree," said Donna. "Let's order room service!"

"No problem," added Pam. "If my credit card limit isn't maxed out, I'll spring for it."

We found the room service menu, made our choices, and Pam called. Twenty minutes later, breakfast was wheeled into our room. The waiter pulled up some chairs, and we chowed down in earnest. Shortly after emptying the coffeepot, Donna suggested we check the weather, and she called the front desk. Hanging up the phone and looking in the direction of the window, she said, "It's forty degrees, and the forecast is cold and foggy today."

"I'm going to freeze!" squealed Pam.

"I supposed some shopping is in order!" commented Donna. "In the meantime, Pam, why don't you call and surprise Steve Pierce to see if we can visit him."

"Sure," she said. "After I take a shower."

"I'm taking a shower," asserted Pam as she ran off to the bathroom and closed the door. Donna moved over close to me and rested her hand on my knee.

"Do you think we've got time to . . . ?"

"Sure." A few seconds later, the bathroom door opened and Pam came running out for her handbag. She said something about her makeup, picked out a few items, and retuned to the bathroom.

Donna moved closer but stopped abruptly when we heard the phone ring. I picked it up.

"This is the front desk calling just to remind you that check out time is 11 a.m. You need to vacate the room precisely at eleven!" *I'm starting to think that a rendezvous with Donna is not going to happen!*

Pam walked out of the bathroom and sat down on the bed beside the nightstand.

"I need to call Steve before we go."

"Make it quick."

"Okay. I've got his number somewhere."

While Pam fumbled through her handbag, Donna half-stumbled into the bathroom. She was obviously jet-lagged, and even two cups of coffee didn't help. It wasn't long before she emerged with solely a towel wrapped around her body.

"Wow, do I feel better!" she boasted. *You really, really don't know how good you look as well!*

Pam was now talking on the phone, a great wide grin on her face. "Yes, that's right! We're here in San Francisco! Of course, we'll find a way to visit. Give me your address. It's where? Mill Valley? On a mountaintop? Can you meet us, and we'll follow you? Okay, we'll be at the gas station at noon."

"Let's go!'" I shouted. "We've got to get a rental car and

stop off for some warm clothes." We left the room and were soon in the lobby. I located a concierge and asked him about a car rental agency and a nearby clothing store.

"Hertz is out the front door and one block to the left. The largest Levi's store in America is about seven blocks from here," he gestured. "Just take a right out of the Hertz garage, go five blocks, and make a right turn. It's just up the street on the right."

We hustled out of the hotel, the cold, raw wind ripping right through me. I turned left. A Hertz sign was in view just a block away. *I hope they'll take my credit card. How embarrassing!* I was relieved to find Hertz willing to rent me a Toyota Corolla. I signed the papers, and we drove to the Levi's store. Luckily, I found a parking space close to the entrance.

"Why don't you get a head start in the women's department? I'll be in the men's," I asserted. "We'll meet at the cash registers."

"Fine," responded Donna.

The girls peeled off on the main floor, and I took the stairs to the third level. Following a quick scan of the department, I settled on a pair of brown corduroy jeans and a long-sleeve sweater and changed into them. What a difference from the suit I came in with!

I tore the tags from both and headed to the cash registers to find Donna and Pam waiting for me.

"Our credit cards are maxed out," Pam reported.

"We'll be okay," I said.

Donna, who was holding a pair of sweaters for the girls, looked hopeful. *Okay, let's try my card.* I handed the cashier my price tags and also the sweaters. She rang up the total, took my credit card, and handed it back to me. *So far, so good.*

"I'm sorry, but your card was rejected," she told me.

"Are you certain? Can you call American Express for me?"

I asked. "Sure," she said as she looked at her pad filled with credit card phone numbers. As soon as she called one of the numbers, she handed me the phone. A man's voice answered.

"Yes, I'm out of town and need to purchase some warm clothes. Is it possible to raise my credit limit?" I inquired.

"What's your card number?" he asked. After I told him he replied, "Let's see. Have you recently made charges of $1,200 to Delta Airlines?"

"Yes."

"And a deposit of a hundred and fifty dollars to Hertz Car Rental?"

"Yes."

"Sorry, Mr. Charnack, but you've just made unusually large purchases on top of your normal monthly charges. I can't authorize any additional purchases. You are past your monthly limit.

"But I'm out of town and need additional credit!"

"I can't help you, but have a nice day and thank you for being an American Express card member."

I handed the phone to the cashier and took out my wallet to find Gene Lawson's phone number. Handing it to the cashier, she dialed the number and returned the phone to me.

"Hello?" came Gene's voice.

"Gene, it's R.C.!" I replied.

"Hey, R.C., how's San Francisco?"

"Lots to tell you, Gene. But I need your help. It's freezing here. I need to buy some clothes for the girls, and my Amex card is all maxed out!"

"Ha ha. What do you want me to do?"

"Can you give your credit card number to the cashier? Between Donna and me, our purchases are roughly a hundred dollars."

"I don't know if they'll do that."

I turned to the cashier.

"He can give you a credit card number, right?" She nodded yes. "She told me it's okay, Gene. Please help me out," I pleaded. I handed the receiver back to her.

"Yes," she said. "I'm ready."

She wrote down Gene's credit card number, entered it into her charge machine, and a moment later a receipt printed out. I took the phone from her hand.

"Thanks, G.L.!"

"No problem. Don't forget you've got two girls to keep you warm!" *Right. It's not that I haven't tried!*

We left the store, piled into the car, and started our drive to Mill Valley. As we drove up 19th Avenue, the Golden Gate Bridge came into view. Almost on cue, the fog began to lift and beautiful sunlight washed over the pastel walk-ups along the way. *So much for the cold weather. This is beautiful!* As we crossed the Golden Gate, Pam and Donna looked back, commenting how they could see the bank of fog over parts of the skyline.

"I don't think I've ever seen anything so wondrous!" commented Pam.

"Wondrous? What does that mean?" inquired Donna.

"You know—incredible!."

"Sure," responded Donna.

As soon as we crossed the bridge, we saw signs for Mill Valley. After taking the exit, we drove down a ramp to a corner gas station. There was Steve's SUV waiting for us!

"Are you guys crazy?" he lamented, as we parked the Corolla and walked up to greet him.

"No," I responded. "Just a little insane!"

"Well, follow me. Carly has put together a little snack and is anxious to see you." Carly was Steve's wife.

"Okay, but don't drive like a maniac," I retorted. "I remember those days driving in your SUV on the streets in Fort Lauderdale!"

We slipped into our car and began to follow Steve up a steep hill that branched off to a narrow, winding road. We continued driving until both cars were on an even steeper incline.

"Look up there!" shouted Donna as she pointed to what appeared to be a double-wide mobile home at the crest of the mountain.

"That must be it," responded Pam. I continued to follow Steve up the hill until we parked in a gravel driveway adjacent to the home. Carly was outside waiting for us.

"Here come the weary travelers," she exclaimed.

"Yes, here we are, for just a few more hours," I responded.

"Few more hours?" asked Steve.

"That's right," Pam offered. "We're on a return flight leaving at six p.m."

"You guys are really crazy," offered Steve. *He's right. We're going to have jet lag for a week.*

For the next several hours, we sat in Steve's house, drank wine, and munched on cheese and crackers. I asked him about the radio station he had transferred to.

"It's like I never worked in radio. They are so much more professional here. Do you want to see the property and my plans for a permanent home?" I followed him out of the front door and was first struck by the remarkable view of the city.

"What do you think," asked Steve. "Beautiful?"

"Indeed. " I countered. "Tell me about the house." He led me around the mobile home and told me about an architect he had hired to design the home.

"The plans aren't quite ready yet," said Steve. *Who cares about the house? I could easily live in the double-wide!*

We returned to a house filled with laughter. The wine was having its effect on the girls. Steve offered me a glass, but I said no as I needed to drive through unknown territory to the airport.

Carly brought over a camera to take a picture for all to remember the occasion. "Hold still," she directed.

About 3:30 p.m., Steve told me I'd better start heading for the airport.

"You're about an hour away and need to return the rental car," he informed me.

"Okay, girls, let's get going," I suggested.

"Do you have to go back so soon?" questioned Carly. "We have room here if you want to stay tonight! *Hmmm, this is really tempting. Perhaps I can bunk with Donna!* I thought about it for a second or two but imagined how jet lag might affect us going back to Fort Lauderdale.

"Yes," I replied, "I'm certain we are going to need at least a day to recover!"

"Fine," Carly responded, "but finish up your wine!" With that, the girls took a large gulp of what remained in their wine glasses and stood up.

"Whoa!" declared Pam holding onto the arm of the sofa. "I think I'd better take a break from drinking for a few hours." *Few hours? How about a few days?*

We wished Steve and Carly well and walked toward the car.

"Look at that view!" exclaimed Donna.

"That's why they call it God's country," confirmed Steve.

Steve then gave me simple directions to the airport. We got back into the car, waved good-bye, and headed down the steep mountain. It wasn't long before we were crossing the bridge and heading down U.S. 101 to the airport. The check in at Hertz was a breeze. *I hope they don't "flag" me for my credit card!*

Walking through the airport to our gate, Donna offered, "How about a drink before we take off?"

"Count me out," responded Pam.

"I think I'll wait until we're in the air," I mused. Donna walked over to a bar and ordered a Bloody Mary in a plastic "to go" cup. *Ugh . . . I think I'm going to throw up!*

We arrived at the gate, boarded the airplane, and quickly found our seats. Pam immediately fell asleep. I was also extremely tired and had almost fallen asleep when I peered over to Donna and saw that she was giving me "the look." *Hmm . . . great idea but I'm about to crash and burn! How about a rain check for later?*

I remember falling asleep until the captain announced our final approach to Atlanta. Both of the girls who had been asleep were starting to stir.

"We'll be on the ground in Atlanta in just a few minutes," I said.

"Terrific," offered Pam. "I'm so tired that I'll probably sleep all the way to Fort Lauderdale."

Upon our arrival in Atlanta, we found our gate for the flight to Fort Lauderdale. The flight was uneventful, and we landed in Fort Lauderdale at 2:30 a.m. As we arrived by cab at the parking lot at Bootleggers, I noticed that it was full of cars and the bar was still open.

"I'm going in for a drink," murmured Donna. "Anyone care to join me?"

"No way!" answered Pam. "I'm going home to my nice cozy bed."

It had been twenty-eight hours since I had taken the dare, and we had taken a suicidal drive to the airport. Ten of those hours had been spent flying cross-country. Several were spent sweating over our money situation. And, finally, there were moments when I thought Donna and I were going to hook up. Apparently the fatigue was showing on my face.

"It's okay, R.C.," said Donna. "I'm certain I can find some-one to buy me a drink."

"Are you going to be okay?" I asked.

"Sure. Never felt better in my life. What a trip!"

I began to walk to my car in the parking lot, but on the way I had another thought. It took me directly to the bar and in Donna's direction. I pulled up a stool next to her, and the bartender walked over.

"Two Bloody Marys please. And pour them heavy if you can!"

Chapter 16

BRIDAL FAIR

Bridal Fair was one of the most frustrating and time-consuming promotions ever undertaken by the WAXY staff. The fair's concept was to bring together an array of businesses under one roof to pander retail business from brides-to-be. Ever since its inception in the 1960s, the event had enticed radio ad sales from local businesses. In return for a commercial schedule on the station, clients would receive an area in which to display their wares at the event and a generous number of on-air promotional announcements.

On its own, the idea of gathering an array of retailers at a convenient location and inviting many brides-to-be was brilliant. However, in each case, the station aligned with Bridal Fair was successful in reaching 18 to 34 year old women, a demographic much younger than WAXY's audience. Nonetheless, General Manager Mark Cole, trying to relive his great Bridal Fair sales days at a former station and desperate to increase declining sales, decided to bring the promotion to South Florida.

"This is going to be GREAT!" Mark bellowed convincingly at one of our sales meetings. "I can't wait to see the happy faces of our participating sponsors at the end of the event!"

"Mark!" called out salesperson Barry Katz, "We don't reach that demographic! How can you expect us to sell this program if our audience doesn't include brides?"

Mark responded, "I don't give a rat's ass. Find a way to make this work, or you'll all be working for someone else!"

We all knew this was Mark's last chance to keep his job because both WAXY's audience ratings and sales revenue were in dreadful shape, which explained his harsh response to Barry's objection. Station ratings had been consistently declining during the past two years, sales revenue falling way below target projections.

The "someone else" we might be working for was Mark's reference to a successor, a reality few wanted. Although Mark's casual style may have been unorthodox, he wasn't one for playing corporate gamesmanship and staff members liked him. After finishing his brief pep talk, he retreated into his office and sales manager Gene Lawson stood up at the end of the conference table. "This is how we're going to work it," said Gene. "We're going to divide up target advertisers—florists, tuxedo shops, travel agents, furniture stores, rental communities, and bridal stores. Rick, you've already made inroads at Susan's Brides. Let's target them to produce the fashion show." The fashion show was the highlight of the five-hour event. It featured a thirty-minute, bridal-gown runway show to present a sponsor's bridal gowns. Naturally, the largest such store in the area, Susan's Brides, was at the top of my list, as it had the best opportunity to benefit from the Bridal Fair gown show.

The owner of Susan's Brides, Bill Schwartz, was a shrewd businessman but an appalling human being. His reputation for "bleeding" suppliers was second only to his obnoxious scoundrel-like personality. If he could have something for free, he'd get it. It had been rumored that Bill had dropped an entire line of gowns when the company had pressured him to pay a past due bill.

When I first contacted Bill, he was particularly interested in the show but ever so frugal about committing the dollars necessary to run a schedule of ads on the station. As we neared the cutoff for sponsors and with no bridal store committed to a package and bridal show, it became clear Bill was going to get what he wanted: a free ride.

Two weeks before the event, Mark Cole called a meeting of the sponsors and sales staff in one of the ballrooms at the Diplomat Hotel in Hollywood, the location of the event. The sales team maintained its professional decorum, dressed in suits and ties, and greeted sponsors at the door. Bill Schwartz arrived and immediately headed for the free Danish and coffee. I had to pry him away to hear Mark's address.

Shockingly, Mark showed up in slacks, cowboy boots, an open polo shirt, and a very worn brown leather jacket. It was an outfit befitting his days living in rural California. He might have also been mistaken as a hotel guest from Texas.

"I want to welcome y'all to the Diplomat Hotel, the site of WAXY's Bridal Fair," Mark said. I'm certain you've had a chance to coffee-up and have a Danish." I glanced at Bill Schwartz, who was nodding his head and slamming down his second Danish, this one of the apricot-filled variety.

"I want to take this opportunity to introduce Bill Schwartz, owner of Susan's Brides, who will handle all of the details of the gown show," Mark explained. He pointed in the direction of the coffee and Bill smiled, pieces of apricot spilling down his chin.

"Please talk with Bill or Rick Charnack this morning about how you can take part in the show." *Who, me? Please don't drag me into this!* "Now here's a diagram of the room. It identifies where your display space will be located."

The small crowd quickly moved to the table where Mark had unrolled the layout. Several loud, dissenting voices could be heard. "I don't want that booth. It's too far from the entrance." "You put me in a corner?" protested another.

In a short time, Mark had a frenzy on his hands. Quite a number of sponsors were unhappy about their location, and he had to do something about it fast.

"I'm certain your salesperson or sales manager Gene Lawson can help you with relocating your space, if you'd like," Mark offered. "I have full confidence that they can make it work for you. In the meantime, thanks for coming, have a great day, and I'll see you here in two weeks!"

Mark quickly exited the ballroom, leaving the WAXY sales team to handle what was becoming an almost riotous situation. The salespersons on hand moved quickly to assuage the negativity coming from their advertisers. Several location changes were made.

Thankfully, the merchants I had sold, other than Bill Schwartz, were now somewhat content with their locations. But Bill was out of control.

"Who was that guy with the leather jacket and Texas drawl?" he jabbered, as white pieces of cheese Danish came spitting out of his mouth. How can I have any confidence with your station when it's run by a cowboy? I've become very concerned about whether or not your station can pull off this promotion. In fact, if you want a bridal show, you can find the models to wear the dresses."

"You know that's not what we discussed," I countered, astonished at this new wrinkle since Bill had agreed over a month ago to procure models for the show.

"That may not be what we discussed, but that's the deal. It's up to you to find the models. You can try Lander Fashion College. They're always looking for modeling opportunities." *Perfect . . . free this and free that. Thanks for the "free tip," schnorer!*

The next day I rushed into the office, called Lander College, and spoke to the modeling director, Susan Orwitz. It turned out that she was a fan of the station and was very accommodating, asking questions about the quality of the event and, of course, the fashion show. But when I mentioned Bill Schwartz's name, she stopped in mid-sentence.

"You really want me to work with Bill Schwartz?" she protested.

"Why?" I replied, knowing that another horror story was coming.

"I've done a few shows with him and he can be difficult at times," she answered. *Oh boy, another body washed up on the shore from Bill's wake.*

I assured her that our management would take care of Bill if he acted up and proceeded to present a detailed proposal including the timetable necessary to produce the event and an option for her to emcee the show. I assured her that everything was above board. She would work directly with Bill—with our tight leash on him—to set up the show and to have six girls at the Diplomat Hotel ballroom on Saturday by 10:00 a.m.

Several days later, she called and agreed to do the show. She had picked out a group of modeling students that were more "mature looking" and promised that they would be at least twenty-one. I was relieved to hear the good news.

Shortly after I concluded making the bridal show plans, my phone rang.

"Rick, it's Bill Schwartz. I've decided to change the time of the show," he advised. "I can't organize the gown collection in time." *Here he goes again with another nonsense excuse!*

"But, Bill, it's too late! The program is already printed, and we're promoting the show on the air. We can't move things around!"

"Rick, either we do it my way or I won't be there."

A number of WAXY sellers in the bullpen were now aware

of my angst. Even Mark Cole, who was walking by, overheard my frustration. Upon hearing me say Bill's name, he rushed to my desk. Just as I was about to tell Bill where he could put his gowns, Mark stepped in and took the phone from me.

"Bill, you know that we've done everything to accommodate you so far," Mark said. "Changing the plan at this point will not be possible. If you want to be in Bridal Fair, you're going to need to be flexible." *Bill, flexible?* For several moments, Mark held the phone, apparently listening to Bill's diatribe. He then gave it back to me and smiled. I held it up to my ear.

"Okay, Rick, we'll do it your way. I'm prepared to go ahead with my part."

"Bill, you know we want to make certain you have a great show," I offered. *Geez, we're giving you a free ride!*

Ironically, the WAXY sales team persevered and came through with a successful event. The team signed up many new advertisers. Sales Manager Gene Lawson convinced a champagne distributor to buy a radio schedule and offer tastings at the event. The ever-present Women's Answers Abortion Clinic bought a sponsorship, theorizing that young marrieds should know their options. My list of sponsors included a leather furniture store, Leather Contempo, managed by a sharp young guy, Dave Mussbaum, with whom I'd established a great relationship. I also sold a sponsorship to The Suburbs, a cluster of rental apartments in the Fort Lauderdale area. The Suburbs was part owned and managed by Rob Shapiro, a shrewd real estate developer. Everything about him spelled "conservative," including his blue blazer, penny loafers, and tortoise-shelled glasses. Rob was fairly quiet during the original briefing and left shortly after Mark's presentation.

The Saturday morning of Bridal Fair arrived, and Bill started in on me first thing. "These girls are entirely too young, and the changing area you've set aside is much too small," he griped.

"Bill, calm down," I countered. "It's not like they were birthed yesterday!" It was true that Lander had sent girls that looked much younger than the "mature" girls we had been promised.

I located Susan Orwitz. "Susan, you promised models in their twenties, not teens!" I declared. "Bill's fuming! What happened?"

"My older girls were unexpectedly committed to a show in Orlando and weren't available," she said. "I think we can pull off a good show with these models. After all, he's not paying for them." *She had a point.*

Bill apparently overheard our conversation and walked over. "What's with the changing area?" he asked. "Your dressing area was constructed in a small corner area of the ballroom!" After listening to his continuous rants and raves, I became desperate and convinced Gene Lawson to give up one of the guest rooms the Diplomat had given us so that the models might change in a more "private" environment. I took a deep breath after I brought Bill the good news. But he was relentless.

"What's with the champagne, Rick?" Bill asked. "I don't want anyone attending my bridal show intoxicated." *Geez . . . this guy has an ego the size of California!*

"No problem," I responded. "Gene Lawson has assured me that we have installed measures that will prohibit attendees from being overserved."

"Okay, but be careful you don't spill any champagne on my gowns or else you'll buy them," he avowed. *Oh, God, this day couldn't end soon enough!*

For the most part, Bridal Fair went off without a hitch. An estimated three hundred fifty brides-to-be and their family members attended. The Landers girls did a fine job of walking the runway to oohs and aahs from the crowd. Between snares and grunts, Bill lit up like a pumpkin when his gowns were showcased.

"Great gowns, huh, Rick?" he gloated. "That's why we're the best!"

"Sure you are," I lied. "You're making the Landers models look like goddesses."

Naturally there were glitches, such as the sound system not working for the first half of the show and an advertiser not showing up (and leaving his display space bare). But in the end, we were proud of what we accomplished for Mark Cole and our team. As soon as the last of the attendees had departed and to celebrate our success, Gene broke open a bottle from the remaining cases of champagne in one of our guest rooms.

I was still in the ballroom and watched as Bill Schwartz collected his belongings and took a parting "shot."

"Rick, this clearly didn't live up to my expectations. I bet you guys are making a fortune from all of your sponsors," cried Bill.

"I thought it went off fairly well," I responded. "Your bridal show was clearly the highlight."

"Highlight? Those Lander girls were a real pain in the ass."

With that he turned and walked away. *Why don't you climb down into the hole you came from?* I then assisted Susan Orwitz in rounding up her girls. Only three of the six were close by.

We searched the hall and the changing room and were unable to find the others. I offered to find transportation home for the three girls that were unaccounted for.

"I'm certain they are in good hands," I said. "We take full responsibility for their safety."

"Okay," she replied, "but make certain they are back in the dorm no later than 10 p.m."

I retreated to the changing room to again look for the girls, and it was unoccupied. I walked down the hall to one of our guest rooms and discovered that the first bottle of champagne had made the rounds of the sponsors and models to toast our success. *So this is where the three models were hiding!*

We popped another bottle and filled everyone's glass. It wasn't long before many of us became unglued. I looked around and noticed that a few of the models and customers had disappeared. Someone told me that the girls had decided to get some fresh air and had gone for a walk on the beach. Much to my dismay, Rob Shapiro had been seen walking off with one of them.

As I was ready to spread my panic around the remaining people in attendance, Leather Contempo's manager approached me.

"I'd like to show you my appreciation for all that you've done, Rick," he said. "Do you have a moment to stop by the room where my friend Lisa and I are staying? It's where you'll see what I brought to the show for the after party. I think you'll like it."

Unwilling to disappoint a customer and relieved to have Bill Schwartz out of my life, I obliged and followed them up to their room. My memory is vague as to what happened next, but I'm fairly certain that I consumed quite a variety of intoxicants. In short order, I was in a haze, barely recognizing my client and his girlfriend.

"We're getting ready to do some heavy partying here, Rick. Would you like to spend the night here with us?"

"Uh . . . oh . . . I've got to be going," I murmured. "Somebody help me up!"

"You're certain you don't want to spend the night here?" Lisa asked with a flirtatious smile.

"Thanks, but I need to check on a client."

"Okay, your call, " she said. "Do you think you can make it back downstairs?"

I tried standing and needed to brace myself on the night-stand. I stumbled out of the room into the hallway, miraculously found the elevator, and rode it down to the first floor. Even in my intoxicated condition, I made it into the ballroom, hoping to find someone to share a late night bottle of champagne with. Just as my luck appeared to run out, I spotted Jill, a blonde-haired WAXY salesperson who was famous for her cute smile and buxom body. She told me that the party had just ended. Most who remained had either gone to bed or were now on the beach feeling very sick.

"Are there any beds left?" I mumbled.

"There's one in my room, and you can share it with me, Rick," she offered. "But you'll have to behave and keep your hands to yourself!"

I told her that I would respect her womanhood. When we arrived at her room, I jumped into bed, looked at my watch, and saw that it was almost 3:00 a.m. The evening's "cocktails" had left me in a stupor, so I quickly fell asleep.

The next thing I remember was being rudely awakened as Jill threw my arm back over to my side of the bed. She obviously didn't appreciate my spontaneous showing of affection during her slumber and remained true to her warning.

"Do that one more time, and I'll cut off one of your body parts," she promised.

I rolled over and fell back into a deep sleep, dreaming of a blonde mermaid with a huge bust.

When I awoke, it was 8:30 a.m., and trouble awaited me. Gene Lawson was pounding on our door. I heard him shout, "Rick, we've got trouble. Several models are unaccounted for! Better get up so that we can start searching."

"Oh no! I personally assured Susan Orwitz that we would guarantee their safety, Gene. We need to get this under control!"

I jumped out of bed with a screaming headache and opened the door. Gene recapped his recent conversation with Susan Orwitz. She had contacted him with news that her models hadn't checked in by their curfew and were missing. He had begun to knock on doors to wake the staffers who had stayed overnight and see if the girls had decided to spend the night in one of our guest rooms.

We dashed to the ballroom and met four other salespersons who had been awakened. Fanning out in groups of two, we further searched the display area and guest rooms. We found two of the girls fast asleep in one of the rooms. A hotel employee, assigned to help us with Bridal Fair, was asleep in a bed with one of them.

We quickly regrouped. Two down, one to go. We tried the restaurants and public areas and again searched the spacious lobby. Only a hotel employee was there, vacuuming the floor. No luck.

A hotel guest, who overheard our dilemma, approached us.

"Why don't you check the pool area and the beach?" he suggested.

We moved on to the pool deck. It was early and fairly deserted. I scanned the beach and, suddenly, observed two figures walking toward the hotel. One was our last lost model, and the other was Rob Shapiro from Suburban Homes! The conservative, soft spoken, father of two was stumbling toward us with his shirt unbuttoned and untucked. Our innocent model had transformed from the angelic bride-to-be to a disheveled teen who had been out all night drinking champagne. Her dress was a mess, sand and dried-out saltwater had turned her gown into a texture resembling paper maché. *Here's one for you, Bill! You deserve it!*

To further punctuate the scene, a champagne bottle was

hanging from her right hand, in an almost poetic pose while she held Rob Shapiro's hand in the other. As they approached me, I could see that Rob was shocked and disoriented.

"Has anyone seen my glasses?" he asked, squinting outward across the beach. "I can't find them."

"Why don't you look in your shirt pocket," Gene said, laughing. "I think they might be in there."

Rob reached into the pocket of his pale-blue button-down shirt and miraculously pulled out a mangled pair of specs. They were bent far beyond repair and missing a lens.

"I guess I'll have to get a ride home," he murmured. "No one will ever believe this! And all of you should forever forget it!"

Gene and I rolled our eyes and laughed. Who would believe that he had spent the evening on the beach with a nineteen-year-old drinking champagne, rolling around in the sand, and busting up his glasses?

Gene quickly retreated to contact Susan Orwitz and share the good news that all models were safe. Grateful for our good fortune, we woke those who were still sleeping and found our way out of the hotel, hung over from champagne, but intact.

Following the Bridal Fair debacle, I never spoke with Rob Shapiro again and assumed he was too embarrassed to take my calls. To this day, whenever I reminisce about Bridal Fair, what comes to mind is a vision of a thirty-five-year-old corporate executive with smashed eyeglasses and a nubile college model stumbling up the beach, empty champagne bottle in hand. Who would ever conceive that it might happen at a promotion that included innocent models: WAXY's Bridal Fair? And who would ever believe that the three cases of empty champagne bottles, lined up in one of the Diplomat's hallways were a byproduct of a promotion appealing to brides-to-be?

Part 2

THE "HIGH" EIGHTIES

Chapter 17

TIME TO MOVE ON

As the 1970s came to a close, my responsibilities as WAXY's regional account executive started to include helping several members of the sales staff. WAXY's local sales manager at the time, Ron Barclay, had a style that was short on creativity and I was often called on as a resource for conceptual selling strategies. As a result of my ideas, even my novice managing skills were helping to close sales. I had conversed with WAXY's general sales manager (my boss) about a possible timetable to sales manager (even co-sales manager,) but had been turned down on a number of occasions. Realizing that the sales management position was not in my immediate future, I began to pursue opportunities outside the company in the Miami market.

In the past, I had been courted by Syd Stone, the general sales manager at Miami's WINZ and WINZ-FM, but at the time hadn't been ready to make a move. However, in the spring of 1980, with a breath of confidence from "coaching" at WAXY, I contacted Syd to inform him that I would be open to considering a sales management position at his stations. Based on this new information, he hastily arranged a meeting for us with his (boss) General Manager Hank Farmer.

With directions to the station in hand, I began the drive

from east Fort Lauderdale to western Dade County, the location of the stations. Although I had been living in western Broward County for many of my years in South Florida, it hadn't prepared me for driving even farther west, practically into the Everglades. *I hope this drive is worth it.*

Upon my arrival, Syd welcomed and walked me into Hank's office. Hank was a large man, overweight, wearing a pale blue Guayabera shirt that effectively hid his protruding abdomen. If I hadn't known better, I would have assumed that he was a well-known fixture on the dominos circuit in Miami's Little Havana. Having spent my early years at a national renowned radio company, Hank's casual demeanor seemed a far cry from the corporate etiquette and sharp business attire to which I had grown accustomed. He seemed like a nice guy, but I wondered how he might have gotten as far as he did in the business. I later found out that he had been a successful sales manager at the former rock-formatted station. A soon-to-be "rabbi" of mine, Don Cahn, who had been general manager, promoted him to this position.

By a stroke of good luck, and my need to justify my long drive to the "swamp," I shortly consummated a deal with Hank and Syd to work as their new business manager. I was flattered by their offer and was ready to make the move immediately. All that was left to do was resign my position at WAXY, something that I feared based on the solid relationship I had with my boss, Gene Lawson. Gene had been an inspiring leader and teacher, so jumping ship wasn't something I looked forward to doing. I owed him a debt of gratitude for his tutelage.

I drove the long distance back to the station and walked directly into Gene's office. Based on the serious look on my face, I could tell he knew something was up, and he asked me to shut his office door.

I sat down and said, "I'm leaving WAXY, Gene. We've talked about managing being the next career step for me and I've secured a sales manager position so that I can continue my growth in the radio business."

Gene leaned back in his chair with a smile on his face. "C'mon, Rick. Are you certain you want to do this? Besides, what type of manager are you going to be?" (I was WAXY's top biller, so his reply didn't surprise me.)

"I'd rather not say, " I replied, being coy as not to expose my move to a competitor.

"Okay, I accept that. But you know how rumors quickly spread in this business."

"I know, but I'd rather not announce my new job until I've officially left WAXY."

"Okay, then, when are you planning on leaving?"

"I'll give you two weeks if you need it, but you and I both know how it works. Now that I've announced my resignation, you'll probably want me to quickly leave the premises. So it's up to you."

"Rick, you've been an important member of the WAXY staff, so I'm not about to escort you out the door this afternoon."

"Good. I'd rather stay until I've contacted my customers and thanked them for their business." *Actually, I'd like to let them know where they can reach me so that they can buy time on my new station.*

Gene laughed. "No, Rick, I don't want you to spend time on the phone calling your customers. Let me inform Norm— our general manager—of the news, and meantime we can officially inform the staff."

I was relieved that the meeting had gone so well with less angst than anticipated. Gene seemed happy for me. *Or was this the lack of emotion managers displayed when an employee decided to leave the company?*

Shortly after our meeting, the following e-mail was circulated to the staff:

TO: WAXY Staff
FROM: Norm Beeman and Gene Lawson
RE: Rick Charnack

It is with much sadness that we announce that WAXY's Regional Account Executive, Rick Charnack, has tendered his resignation effective immediately.

Rick was one of the original WAXY staff members and has been responsible for much of our sales success throughout the years. As regional sales executive over the past three years, Rick has sold many prestigious accounts, such as Independent Life Insurance, Canada Dry, Eastern Airlines, and Publix Supermarkets.

Rick has accepted a management position at a Miami area radio station, which he will announce at a later date.

Please help us to thank Rick for his contribution to our success with a toast at Uncle Funny's tomorrow at 5:00 p.m.

Norm and Gene

I'll never forget my last day on the job. At 5:00 p.m., nearly all of the WAXY staff gathered with Carl and Norm at Uncle Funny's, a lounge/restaurant directly across the street from the station.

After a few rounds of drinks, Norm made an obligatory salute by presenting me a framed copy of the cover of an SRDS (Standard Rate and Data) publication. The voluminous "book" was a monthly publication that contained the rates of each station in America, by market. Our company had reserved an advertising space on the cover each December so that it could showcase its high-achieving talent, among them the best company salesperson. Those sellers—from all of the company stations—who had achieved 100 percent of their annual sales budgets were listed. Above those listed, at the top of the page, was an area identifying Superior Achievers, an elite group of managers, salespeople, and programmers from stations throughout America who had truly given 110 percent of themselves. My name was among them.

Gary held up the framed cover for all to see.

"Thank you, Rick Charnack, for your contribution to our success," said Norm. "You've been a big part of WAXY's growth throughout the five years you've been here, and we wish you the best of luck."

Gene chimed in, "Rick has accepted a position with a radio company in Miami but has decided to keep it confidential." *Damn right. I'm not going to give you a head start protecting the accounts I'm planning to take with me.* "However, I'm certain we'll see you in the market, right, Rick?"

"Absolutely," I replied. "I look forward to some friendly competition."

Excited about my new opportunity and not wanting to linger, I finished my drink and thanked Carl, Norm, and my fellow staffers for their gesture and started to head for the door. Just as I was about to exit, Carlie Carl, one of WAXY's on-air personalities, approached me.

"I know there's a policy about never fooling around with anyone in the company, Rick. But now that you're gone, how about coming over to my apartment for my own personal send-off?"

"Right now?" I inquired.

"Right now," she confirmed. "My apartment is five minutes away, so follow me."

Carlie was someone with whom I had often flirted, but I never got past the gesture. She was beautiful: brown eyes, flowing brown curly hair, slender, and a very sexy voice, the type that listeners might often fantasize about.

"C'mon, let's go," I said, and we both exited the restaurant.

I drove away with mixed emotions. WAXY had been my first "family" in the business, and those who have worked in radio can truly appreciate what a first "family" represents in their career.

My sad thoughts, however, were quickly squelched by the thought of Carlie's invitation to join her at her apartment. Besides, what better way to begin a two-week hiatus from the business? My WAXY days might have been over, but my new beginning was already reaping big rewards!

Chapter 18

THE WINZ STATE OF MIND

When compared to my career experience at Metro Radio, the environment of the WINZ-AM and I-95 FM (WINZ-FM) stations gave new meaning to the word *bipolar*. On one hand, there existed a once successful all-news station that had once dominated the format category but was suffering from audience erosion because of a copycat station, WNWS. The station had suffered a major loss of both on-air announcers and prestige when its competitor hit the airwaves.

On the other hand, an up-and-coming FM station—I-95—was experiencing a ratings explosion in the pop music radio genre. Most of the company staff and financial support had shifted to promoting the new product. Hence, one station was on its way up, and the other was struggling and on the way down.

After a short time on the job, my observation was that nothing fazed General Manager Hank Farmer. He spent hours alone in his office and frequently took afternoons off to spend time with his fiancée. When the word that he was acquiring a station in southern California circulated our confines, his lack of interest in our affairs made sense. It was obvious he had one foot out the door.

The official word of his leaving finally came down in a hastily assembled staff meeting in the company's atrium, an area with overhead skylights that had been designed so that plants might receive a lathering of afternoon sunlight. We all crowded into the space, several standing in the vegetation to hear Hank's speech.

"I'm here to announce that I'm leaving the company," Hank said. "As most of you are aware, both Lisa (his fiancée) and I are moving to California where I'm going to be the proud owner of a station."

"How soon?" asked Joe Power, WINZ's production director.

"Oh, I see," countered Hank. "Can't wait until I'm out the door, huh?" *Truthfully, I haven't seen much of your time inside our doors.*

"Well," continued Hank, "just two weeks. And I'm pleased to inform you that Syd Stone will be taking over my duties as general manager." A hush suddenly filled the room. *Syd— the new general manager? This guy often loses the keys to his own car!*

I supposed Syd's being named general manager of the stations was a good thing for me. After all, he was the one who had been responsible for my hiring. I was one of "his" people, so my job wasn't in jeopardy. He was also coming around to the philosophy that my business required "merchandising"—or giveaways—to make large sales. However, he didn't miss a chance to remind me that I wasn't working for my former radio corporation and our company didn't have an endless money pit. *I'm now working for a newspaper company from Maine!*

To be of maximum benefit to both stations' sales teams, I created promotional ideas, the all-important sponsor "hooks" that are offered to advertisers and manufacturers to earn their business. They had been a part of my success at WAXY-FM and were critical when selling traditional co-op accounts and achieving the stations' new business budgets. I studied industry publications and brought the most timely campaigns to programming/promotions meetings that were held each week. It was a tough sell. The I-95 programming was committed to a "clutter free" environment and WINZ's "all news" format provided little, if any, promotional announcements. Therefore, my option was to help salespersons bring promotional support to customers in the form of sponsorship identifications that were included in news, traffic, and weather reports.

Only one salesperson put forth an all-out effort to incorporate co-op into his sales repertoire. His name was Lonnie Klein. Lonnie was a heavy-set, six-foot-three-incher with cheek and neck jowls you could get lost in. A chain smoker, he'd walk around the sales office with a cigarette conspicuously dangling from his mouth. His puppy dog appearance aptly complimented his selling skills so that most advertisers couldn't say no to him. He was just a loveable guy.

Lonnie even convinced the WINZ program director to allow him an on-air slot on the news station (which aired talk radio in the evenings and on weekends.) He utilized this slot to sell his own advertisers "live" commercials (voiced by Lonnie on the air) and provided generous two-minute, even three-minute, spots—rather than the standard one-minute commercials he charged for—that would drive Syd crazy. One of his favorite advertisers, Miami Beach Chocolates, would delight each time Lonnie would ramble on about their business while munching on a chewy, fruit-filled piece of homemade candy.

Lonnie enthusiastically used my research to create sales. Accordingly, he was one of my biggest fans and largest producers. In fact, he was singlehandedly responsible for helping me achieve the co-op budget during my first year at WINZ.

In addition to being a talented salesman, Lonnie was a

showman of the first order. He would make sales calls on shopping malls with creative ideas that were always special. In fact, it was on one of these calls that I accompanied him to a strip mall in his Cadillac, the front seat reclined almost to the trunk to accommodate his less than svelte body. We arrived at the shopping plaza in Lauderhill and pulled up to a vacant store with a large paper sign designating "Leasing Office" in the window.

"Let me do the talking, Rick," Lonnie said. "I've word that the center is trying to fill empty storefronts and has set aside marketing dollars."

Lonnie opened the driver's-side door, which groaned as if it were tired from his constant tonnage. He leaned on the door and pulled out his tan briefcase. I followed along as he walked through the storefront door.

"Hi, sweet thing," he said to a girl in her early twenties who was sitting on a folding chair at a metal desk near the front door. "We're here to see Ann Comacho."

"And who should I say is calling?"

"Tell her Lonnie Klein and Rick Charnack.

"Well, she's on the phone right now."

"We'll wait."

"Okay. Have a seat over there by the coffee maker."

"Sweet Thing" pointed us to several metal folding chairs lined up against the same wall as a folding card table with a Mr. Coffee on top. As we walked over, Lonnie pointed in Ann's direction and half-whispered in my ear.

"There she is. She's quite a looker, huh?"

"Geez, Lonnie, she almost heard you!"

We sat down and gazed around the room. By all appearances, the space had never been filled. Fresh plasterboard walls, a bare concrete floor, and an unfinished ceiling confirmed that it was a brand-new center. Ann was seated in the back of the room behind a desk with what appeared to be blueprints for the center on the wall next to her. Lonnie was right. She looked professional . . . too professional to be sitting in an empty strip mall storefront. She was put together well—dark short styled black hair that folded down just past her neck, white chenille blouse, blue blazer, and a black soft leather business case on top of the desk.

We sat for about ten minutes while she was on the phone until Lonnie couldn't stand it any longer. He stood and walked over to visit with "Sweet Thing."

"What's your name?" he asked.

"Laurie," she responded.

"That's a pretty name, doll."

"Thanks."

"How long have you been working here?"

"I've worked with Ann for about a year. We opened the center in Coral Springs together."

"You mean the one on Riverside?"

"That's right. What station are you with?"

"WINZ."

"Oh, the all-news station."

"That's right. I'm a radio star." *Here it comes. . . .*

"Really! What show?"

"The Lonnie Klein Show. You should come to the station sometime, and I'll put you on the air. You've such a pretty voice." *Oh boy!*

"Laurie," came a voice from behind the rear desk. "You can send back Lonnie now."

I stood and walked over to Ann's desk. Lonnie scooted over to where we had been seated, grabbed his briefcase, and walked up behind me. I was the first to reach Ann, so I extended my hand and said, "Hi, Ann. I'm Rick Charnack."

"Hello, Rick. I assume that's Lonnie behind you. Hi,

Lonnie. I'm Ann Comacho," she said, standing up from her chair. "Why don't you both sit down?" She pointed to two folding chairs in front of her desk.

"Hi, Ann," responded Lonnie. "Thanks for seeing us. As I mentioned, Dave Levine at the corporate office suggested we come in and see you to show you an advertising plan for the center."

"That's great, Lonnie, but we don't believe in media advertising. We rely on real estate partners and tenants to spread the word. But you must have done a great sales job with Dave, and he asked me to speak with you. So what's this I hear about a station appearance?"

"Well, I don't know how much you know about the station, Ann, but we reach over three hundred thousand persons in Broward County each week. Many of those are adult residents living in communities near your center." *There's no factual evidence to that point!*

I jumped in, "Ann, we do reach adults, age forty-five and older in the county. The most recent ratings confirm that they represent many businessmen who listen for our news and weekend programming and a healthy percentage in your trading area."

"That's right, Ann," Lonnie added.

"So what do you have for me?"

"A very exciting promotion!" Lonnie expounded, moving forward in his chair. *Look out! This guy might fall out of his chair, and that would be catastrophic considering his weight.*

"As you know, Ann, I have a large audience during my Saturday afternoon show on WINZ. I receive hundreds of calls each week from listeners particularly between two and four p.m. I'm going to do something special for you. In fact, it's something that's never been done before!" *Sure . . . wanna buy a watch?*

"You ready for this?" Lonnie asked, standing up.

"Okay . . . I guess so," Ann responded, backing up her chair.

"I'm going to bring my show here on Saturday and broadcast from your center!"

"Really? And you actually believe that your weekend show will draw attention to the stores here and potential lessees?"

"Well, you haven't heard the best part!" *Okay . . . here it comes.*

"As you know, the Capp Brothers Circus is in town. They have set up their show tent at the Sunrise Fair and will be doing shows over the next few weeks. The exciting news is that I own two elephants—Lenore and Daisy—that are on loan to Capp Brothers. I've made arrangements to have them here, at your center, during my show! Can you imagine the crowds that will be here to see my girls?!"

"Wait a minute," sputtered Ann. "You intend to bring two elephants here? Who's going to take care of them while you are on the air? What happens if they crap all over my property?"

"That's easy. I'll make certain that a handler from the circus is here at all times. In fact, Lenore and Daisy are so tame, we can probably offer rides to those who attend the promotion."

"No friggin' way, Lonnie. You're pushing the envelope. I'm all for creating a promotion that will yield us results. The station broadcast seems like a good idea. But I'm not sold on having two defecating elephants and a liability case on my property."

"So we don't offer rides. But think of all the publicity your center will receive from having elephants in your parking lot. I guarantee it!" *This pitch is now out of control. Lonnie's living up to his reputation as doing anything for a sale and trying the patience of a prospective client!*

I couldn't hold back and decided it was time to break into his presentation. I stood up and blurted out, "Don't you agree that Lonnie's promotion is really one of a kind? He's going to put his all into making it work, even bringing elephants here! However, the Capp Brothers are going to be in town only for another few weeks, so time is of the essence. Why don't you and Lonnie work out a schedule to reach both our news and weekend listeners so we can start promoting the event on the air as soon as possible?"

"Wait!" retorted Ann. "Not so fast, Rick. How much is this going to cost me?"

"Way less than what it's worth," piped up Lonnie. "It shouldn't be more than $8,000 for everything, including commercials, my remote broadcast, circus, and other fees."

"You know, Lonnie, it's a good thing that you were recommended by Dave Levine and he's open to suggestions to use WINZ. Otherwise, I might think you were crazy. I suppose I need to trust that you wouldn't steer me wrong. Why don't you bring back a proposal for me to have him sign off on it?"

"Better yet," Larry countered, "I live right around the corner from Dave's office, so I'll drop off a copy to both of you." *Good move, Lonnie. Make certain you're maintaining contact with the final decision maker.*

"Fine," responded Ann, somewhat reluctantly. "Get back to me tomorrow."

"You got it!" bellowed Lonnie.

"Nice to meet you, Ann," I said, standing up.

"Same here, Rick. Please keep Lonnie on a short leash until all of the details are worked out."

"That won't be a problem, Ann," responded Lonnie. "I think we're all on the same page."

Lonnie stood and shook Ann's hand. We walked to the

front door, and Lonnie offered a farewell to Laurie. "Nice to meet you, sweetie."

Lonnie returned and closed the deal for $8,200. With the help of a crackerjack engineering department, he set up a remote broadcast on the arranged day to broadcast his show. Daisy made an appearance with a handler from the Capp Brothers Circus. Most of the hundred-plus persons who made their way to the shopping plaza weren't there to see Lonnie eat chocolates on the air but to pet Daisy's trunk. She cooperated fully by not making a mess in the parking lot.

Ann was pleased that most of the retailers experienced enhanced sales from the event. To top it off, a lease was signed for an empty storefront.

And Lonnie continued to go to any length to put new retail dollars on the station—even if it included bringing out elephants to close the deal.

Chapter 19

TO FIRE OR NOT TO FIRE

There came a time—or several for that matter—when I found it necessary to terminate an underperforming salesperson. I suppose that's a kind way of saying it was necessary for me to fire someone.

Following my promotion to local sales manager at I-95 FM, I inherited a group of salespersons, some of whom had been on board prior to the station changing its format. In its prior incarnation, the station had reached a pinnacle of ratings success as an album rock station, Zeta4, but had taken a significant ratings dive as the station's uniqueness fizzled out. (In addition to the migration of South American residents, the *Mariel* boatlift created an influx of Spanish-speaking Miamians who were fond of Latin rather than rock music.)

When a station's ratings are so high as to create a huge advantage over its competition, orders for commercial time are almost automatic. For instance, business from advertisers such as soft drink companies can often be negotiated by telephone without leaving the station. One salesperson had become adept at telephone sales but found his billing shrinking, along with the ratings, because he seldom left the office to make new sales calls as the station's ratings were falling. His name was Warren Ruskin.

As one of the top billers at rock station Zeta4, Warren had

settled into a comfort zone. His daily routine was to show up for work at his own convenience. Once he arrived, he would read the newspaper, converse with other employees, and make a few phone calls, including one to his girlfriend du jour. The majority of telephone calls were made to accounts that I insisted he call on and not of his own volition.

During the years I worked at WAXY, to stem the tide of account erosion, I had been trained to make as many face-to-face sales contacts on new advertisers each day as possible. In fact, even when faxing became the way to do business, I continued to preach it religiously. No, let me correct that. Even when doing business by fax changed the way we did business, I continued to stress the value of getting in front of a client. It was my belief that making calls in person made it harder for the client to say "no" and, as important, one might uncover an opportunity before it was open for bid by other stations.

For the most part, Warren avoided this important part of radio sales. In addition, while most of us took great pride in our appearance by donning flattering clothing, Warren pointed out how he would only "dress for success" during his evenings carousing at clubs. *So much for priorities, right?*

I approached Warren one afternoon at his desk while he was reading the newspaper.

"What do you have planned for today?" I asked.

"I'm waiting for a call from our largest soft drink account," he responded.

"What do you expect?"

"I'm hoping for more money—a larger schedule."

"Have you pitched for more business?"

"No. She loves me and will probably give me more money."

"How much has she given you this year so far?"

Warren opened his file drawer and papers flew everywhere. "Let me see."

Somewhat shocked by his disorganization, I covered up my surprise with a chuckle when I observed his filing system.

"What are you doing, Warren? The contracts for your largest account are stuffed into your drawer? Have you any idea what she is spending?"

"It's about ninety thousand dollars."

"*About* ninety thousand dollars? What if she called and asked you to give her an accounting of the account's spending history?"

"Oh, that's easy. I would have Barbara (our secretary) do it for me." *Oh, I see. Now he's got a private assistant!*

"I think it would be a good idea for you to know what she's spending without making a special project for Barbara," I said.

Stunned, I turned and walked back to my office. I found no comfort in the realization that one of our largest accounts was managed by a lackadaisical salesperson. In fact, I wondered how much we might have on the books if Warren were making regular in-person sales calls with his clients.

On this particular occasion, the call from his client never came and Warren was stiffed on a contract that would have added many more thousands of dollars to the annual contract. It had not been a good day for Warren, and a large black mark had been tallied against him in his effort to impress me.

"What happened, Warren?" I asked after the news.

"She got a deal from another station."

Are you certain?"

"That's what she told me."

"When's the last time you saw her?"

"I don't know. Maybe six months ago. But I phone her all the time." *Sure you do. But what does that mean?*

Fuming, I walked back to my office. It was one thing having lost a buy to a competitor, and it was another that it happened because my salesperson was not doing his job. However,

I decided to give Warren another shot and urged him to take his client out to lunch during the following week.

On the following weekend, I visited a disco in a large private club in North Miami Beach. When I arrived, I peered around the room and recognized a familiar face. There, strutting his all on the dance floor was—you guessed it—Warren Ruskin. Warren was wearing what appeared to be an expensive beige suit, dark blue shirt, and paisley handkerchief, an outfit he might have replicated from *GQ*. He saw me standing at the bar and walked over following the end of the song.

"What's up, Rick?" he asked.

"Nice suit, Warren. Haven't I seen you wearing the same one at work?" I responded, laughing.

"Not a chance. This one's a special reserve for my trips to the clubs."

"I see." *Not really! What I see is someone who wears mediocre clothing and waits by his phone for orders.*

"I've got to go to the men's room," he said.

"What are you drinking, Warren? I'm buying."

"Just order me a vodka and grapefruit. I've got a buzz already. Besides, I'm making a trip to the men's room for a different kind of buzz."

I looked into Warren's eyes and noticed how red they were. *What a great impression this guy's making with me!* After a drink, I left the club unhappy with what I had witnessed.

On Monday morning, I implored Warren to contact his buyer and make arrangements for both of us to take her out to lunch. I hadn't met her and, as sales manager, thought it best to see for myself how Warren related to her. The fact that he told me about their "love affair" intrigued me.

After many futile attempts, Warren was unable to arrange a lunch.

"She says she's too busy to stop and take a lunch," he said while lounging in one of my office chairs.

"What about making a sales call?" I inquired.

"Ditto. She's not seeing anyone this week."

I was feeling very uneasy about their relationship and Warren's work ethic in general. Salespersons are either on the way up or on their way down, and he was clearly the latter. I needed to make certain I had someone who wasn't riding on his or her laurels and was representing I-95 FM's new format with verve.

Instinctively, I recognized that Warren wasn't going to be a key piece on my new team and needed to be replaced with someone more tenacious. The decision to fire him was made easily after several interviews with Carol Seiss, an aggressive young salesperson from West Palm Beach. Besides earning a great reputation selling a station with modest ratings, she had the level of confidence and ambition that I was looking for. I crafted a list of accounts, mostly from Warren's list, for Carol to take over. She would become one of the key ingredients of my new local sales team. All that was left for me to do was to fire Warren.

I called Warren into my office late one Friday afternoon. There had been rumors circulating all week that he was going to be fired.

"I'm going to let you go," I started.

"I know," he responded. "I saw this coming several weeks ago."

"So, what are you going to do?"

"Probably take a few weeks off and look for another job, maybe as a manager." *What? Is this guy crazy? He can barely operate as a salesperson!*

"Well," I added, reluctantly, "if you need a reference for what you've done here during the Zeta4 days, I'll give you one."

"That would be great."

"What about your accounts? It might be difficult, but I'd like you to hold off contacting them."

"I've already told a few that I'll probably be fired." *What? What could possibly be the purpose of doing that?"*

"They love me, Rick! I told you that when you became my manager." *Sure. They love you so much that you get stiffed on buys!*

"Terrific."

I could hardly wait to find out what Warren's clients had planned since he was leaving. Would they cancel their schedules? Would they never do business with I-95 FM again? After all, he had been working for the company for four years. *And he had told me they all loved him.*

My fears were quickly allayed when I began to call around to his accounts. Upon telling them I had decided to move forward with a new salesperson, not one was surprised or disappointed. In fact, remember the client who he told me "loved" him? During our telephone conversation, she fed me an interesting tidbit of information that confirmed I had made the right decision to let Warren go.

"It doesn't surprise me," she said. "Warren was one of the laziest salespersons I've ever worked with. In fact, he hasn't been to my office in over two years."

"I'd like to come see you with our new salesperson," I countered.

"Absolutely. I'll make some time available for you, Rick. I'm ready for a breath of fresh air."

I knew I had made the right decision. What I didn't know was that it would be met with such enthusiasm on the part of one of the station's largest accounts.

Several months later, I received a phone call from Warren. He had landed a job as a sales manager at a local station that wasn't a direct competitor. *Can you believe it?*

"Rick, remember the weekly sales planner forms you requested that I always complained about?" offered Warren. "I'm now asking my sellers to complete them. Thanks, Rick."

"You're welcome, Warren. Congratulations on your new job. And good luck in creating love affairs at your new station. I'm certain your clients will find you as lovable as when you were at I-95."

Chapter 20

I-95 . . .
THE NIGHTCLUB STATION

It was a simple premise: Build a pop/dance radio format appealing to Miami's young adults, aged eighteen to thirty-four, and the nightclub business would soon follow. Accordingly, I-95 FM was launched during the era identified with fast cars and faster women as depicted in the television show *Miami Vice*. As local sales manager of I-95, I recognized the opportunity of doing business with nightclubs and set my sights on outsmarting, outwitting, and outselling the competition.

Carol Seiss, who had replaced Warren Ruskin and was one of my early hires, had been breaking sales records at a station in the West Palm Beach market, seventy miles north of Miami. Upon her arrival at I-95, Carol dove into the nightclub business category and, in short order, sold a three-month contract for a Friday evening dance contest at a Fort Lauderdale discotheque.

Shortly thereafter, Carol closed another three-month contract for a Saturday amateur night contest at another Fort Lauderdale club. Although she was on a roll, both contests required her attendance each night and several judges. As luck would have it, one of her committed judges dropped out after the first week.

"Rick," began Carol as she peered into my office, "what are you doing on Friday evenings for the next three months?"

"What's up, Carol?" I responded suspiciously. "Please don't tell me that you've lost a judge. It's only the first week!"

"Rick, you know how hard I've worked for this sale."

"Yes, and you told me you had an iron-clad plan for judges, right?"

"Well, I thought so. But you wouldn't want me to lose the deal, right? Nightclub owners are finicky about radio commitments, and I don't want to take a chance by not having enough judges."

"If it's just for one night, I'll fill in. But please don't count on me for the duration."

"Fine, just be there this coming Friday." *Sure, I'll be there. Nothing like losing one-half of my weekend.*

The first Friday night went smoothly. Carol was superbly buttoned down and had all of the judging rules spelled out as I sat on the stage with her and another judge. Contestants and partygoers were dancing to "Flashdance" in spandex and hairdos that were in permanent curls. Everything she had created was falling into place.

However, the Saturday-night contest at another club turned into a fiasco. One of the problems with ambitious salespersons is that they tend to overextend themselves, especially when it involves station appearances. At the moment she sold both weekend promotions, Carol had little fear that she could pull off both and harvest the commissions that were to come her way. However, that was easier said than done.

Saturday's contest involved amateur singers who were competing for a grand prize of a recording contract. During the very first evening, a contestant charged that the contest was rigged, which prompted a drunken rage aimed at the club owner. As a result of the incident, the unhappy client insisted that the twelve remaining weeks be shut down, forcing cancellation of a lucrative contract.

Following the sales meeting on Monday morning, Carol pulled me into my office to air her frustration.

"Saturday night's contest was a disaster," Carol said, almost sobbing. "A contestant and the owner got into a war of words that almost erupted in a fist fight!" *Great. Now I've advertiser, contestant, and salesperson emotionally unhinged.* "And, to top it off, the owner wants to cancel the promotion after only one week on the air. Since we are already promoting a three-month contest, we can't suddenly cancel it."

It was true. Promotional commercials that included a station endorsement and a grand prize would amount to false advertising if it were suddenly pulled from the airwaves.

"Carol, I'm going to give you a hand here," I said. "But you need to calm down. All is not lost. What time does your client arrive at work?"

"About 3 p.m."

"Call him and let him know that we can be at his club by four o'clock, you've got the attention of your manager, and I'm very concerned about the situation that occurred on Saturday night."

"Fine."

Carol left my office only to return ten minutes later.

"He's reluctantly agreed to see us at four but told me that he was no longer interested in the contest and wants to cancel."

"Okay. I'll come up with a solution by then." *Good luck. These club owners are brutal.*

Attending a meeting at a club during daytime hours can certainly bring out the worst in a usually classy enterprise. The stale smell of cigarette smoke and alcohol can be overwhelming. And what made the club especially eerie were the floodlights that exposed every distressed area that was hidden to the naked eye in the darkness of the club's mood-provoking night lighting. The foul odor and visual defects struck me as I entered the club and walked through the kitchen. *Ugh!*

We arrived at a tiny back office with room enough for a desk, a desk chair, and an additional chair that might be used by any variety of salesmen doing business with the club. I noticed the client engaged in an animated phone conversation, hands flailing, while sizing me up. He finished the conversation and hung up the phone with a loud thud.

"So this is your manager," he said, reaching over and kissing Carol on the cheek. *Nice to see you're on kissing terms with your client.*

"I'm Rick Charnack," I said, reaching out my hand to shake his.

"Tony. Just call me Tony."

I had learned during my years of calling on nightclub managers that they typically conducted their business late in the afternoon over a glass of coffee. "Just Tony" was dressed in wrinkled faded jeans, a wide-open black-and-purple shirt that revealed a sprinkling of hair on his chest, and scuffed white loafers. His greasy head of combed-back hair fell to his shoulders. I guessed his age as forty-five or so.

A man with a loud voice peeked into the office. "Tony, we need ten cases of Michelob. Hi, Carol. Nice to see you."

"Call Stu at Premium and tell him to get the hell over here. They're late on their delivery. And tell him we'll be switching brands if he doesn't get his ass over here." *Terrific. Now it's my turn to walk on the hot coals.*

"Tony, I brought my manager here because he wanted to talk about what happened on Saturday night," offered Carol.

"What's there to talk about, Carol? I'm finished with the contest."

Carol turned to me with puppy-dog eyes, waiting for me

to drop pearls of wisdom on the situation. *At that moment I recalled the look of each salesperson that had "doggy eyes" expecting me to save their ass.*

"Tony, Carol has knocked herself out putting the details of this contest together," I said. "She's been in my office countless hours pleading and working on the on-air promotional announcements that you aren't paying for, an outstanding grand prize that was arranged on your behalf and a very hot idea for drawing new customers to your club."

"What's the point, Rick?" asked Tony. "If the contest is going to create pissed-off customers, why should I spend any money on it? I'd rather spend my money somewhere else."

"The point, Tony, is that you own the best disco in Fort Lauderdale." *As long as the floodlights aren't illuminated.* "I appreciate your business and want to make this right. I've an idea that you're going to like."

"Okay. This better be good."

"I admit that our promotion has started off on the wrong foot. However, it's a concept to introduce new customers to your club. Tell you what, Tony. I'm prepared to take personal responsibility for making certain the promotion goes smoothly."

"What does that mean?"

"It means that I will be here each Saturday night to assist Carol and make certain you never need to step in again."

"See, Tony!" Carol said, jumping out of her chair. "Rick is willing to give up his Saturday nights just to be here at your club to ensure that the contest works." *Don't go too far, Carol. We never, ever want to promise that contests work, especially at a nightclub.*

"So you're promising me that you'll be here every Saturday night?" clarified Tony.

"That's right. You have my commitment to keep things under control."

I could see Tony mulling over his options. The room became eerily silent, and I noticed he looked at Carol.

Finally, he spoke. "Okay, Carol, you win. I'll continue with the promotion as long as Rick keeps his eye on the contestants if they flip out. But if I see you losing control, I'll shut down the contest immediately and ask all of you to leave the premises." *What a gesture! He's bleeding us for more attention in one thought and throwing us out the next.*

"Thank you, Tony! You're the best!" gushed Carol.

"Fine," responded Tony. "Now let me get back to business here."

Carol and I walked out the office door, through the club, and out a side door to my car.

"You were great," she gushed.

"Sure, I just guaranteed my appearance at another three-month nightclub promotion. *And gave up my Saturday nights for the duration. What am I, nuts?*

Assuming that I might prevent rising contestant emotions was a stretch, but I thought it was the only way to keep the business. Carol had been relentless in selling Tony, and I didn't want to see her take a hit. *Oh, the things we'll do for a salesperson and station to help keep a radio order!*

Unfortunately, I attended several additional Friday promotions (Carol took advantage of my offer for "standing in") and Saturday night's contest for the three months. As it turned out, the contest at Tony's bombed due to sparse turnout, and there were moments when I thought I was going insane from the smoke and pathetic performances. Even several glasses of vodka didn't help.

On one of the Saturday nights, a contestant saw me drinking at the bar close to the stage. He identified himself as a station listener and had decided to come to check out the promotion. When I discovered he was a contestant, I decided to buy him a drink. Before long, he was sharing stories about his dream of being a stand-up comic. He suddenly excused himself, and I assumed he had gone to the men's room. When he returned, he leaned over to tell me something.

"Rick, I left a gift for you in the men's room," he said.

"What type of gift?" I asked. *Is this a bribe to advance his chances in the contest?*

"Why don't you find out for yourself?"

Curious, I turned and walked to the men's room. Upon arriving, I shared a brief story about my new "friend" with the attendant and inquired if there might be a "gift" he had left for me.

"He sure did," he said. "Here it is."

The attendant handed me a small plastic bag with a generous amount of white powder in it. I quickly put it in my pocket and left a tip for him.

"Thanks," I heard him say.

I had a clear choice: I could spend the next several hours extremely bored and observing amateur contestants, or I could slip into a stall and sample some of what had been left for me. My better judgment eluded me momentarily. I walked over and closed the door to a stall.

In a matter of minutes, any thought of boredom quickly faded away. More important, the irony that I had given up my Saturday night to support an ambitious member of my sales team quickly took its place.

Chapter 21

GRAB A STRAW AND JOIN ME!

The phone rang in my office one Thursday morning, and I picked it up.

"Rick, this is Sam Crown from the Crown Public Relations Agency."

"Do I know you?" I responded.

"You don't, Rick, but I'm calling on behalf of a friend who's graduating from college in a few weeks. Are you looking for a good salesperson?" *How unusual. This guy's acting as an agent?*

"I may be looking to expand my sales staff, Sam. But I'm not certain why you are contacting me instead of your friend."

"It's because he's an exceptional person, and he's asked me to get the ball rolling for him. I'm going to fax over his résumé so you can see for yourself. When's the best time for him to contact you?"

"Hold on, Sam! I have no idea about your friend. I'd be happy to review his résumé and let you know if I want to meet him. Send it to me and I'll call him if I'm interested."

"Sure, Rick, no problem."

I hung up the phone in amazement. In all my years as a sales manager, I had never had an agent call me to introduce me to his "client." I had to admit, it was a novel approach.

It wasn't long before my assistant walked into my office with Sam's friend's résumé. I was immediately impressed by what I saw. The candidate, Terry Webber, was about to graduate from college and was committed to moving to South Florida and breaking into the radio business. I preferred to train new, inexperienced salespersons, and it appeared that his qualifications were worth a telephone conversation. The following day he contacted me.

"Rick, it's Terry Webber. Sam Crown has spoken to you about me. I've just received my business degree and am ready to start selling radio. Have you an opening?"

"That's fast, Terry. I'm impressed with your quick follow-up. Your resume is impressive, and I'm interested. When are you going to be in town so that we might meet in person? I need to speak with you to more adequately judge whether your qualifications are a good fit for our growing team. And, to answer your question, yes, I'm looking for another salesperson to join my team."

"I can be in town later this week, Rick. How about meeting me on Saturday? My friend has a place in Fort Lauderdale, and I can stay with him."

I really liked this kid. From what I saw on his résumé and the way he conducted himself on the phone, he appeared to be very assertive, but professional—an ideal candidate. I wondered how he might conduct himself in person and was looking forward to meeting him.

We met on Saturday at a restaurant on the waterway. He made a favorable impression with his appearance: short dark hair, blue polo shirt, khaki slacks, brown eyes, a wide grin that communicated a friendly demeanor. On the surface, it was all the assurance I needed to feel confident that I might be able to take him under my wing and train him (the same way my first Florida sales manager, Ken, had done for me.) Terry had nothing standing in his way and assured me that he could pack up and drive down immediately.

During the sales meeting the following week, I announced to the team that I had hired a rookie. It was met with grunts and groans.

"Rick, you already have five salespersons. Why another?" asked Benji Weinstein.

"How many accounts are you going to take away from me?" inquired Pamela Stein.

"Listen up," I said. "We have plenty of room to expand our staff, and I remain committed to making certain no one suffers. Besides, you know we're in the building stages, there's plenty of business for everyone, and I think that bringing in a trainee fresh out of college will complement the team."

I was committed to keeping those hard-working members of the team motivated and without fear of losing account opportunities. It was important to maintain the right chemistry so that we could function as a team rather than a back-stabbing department of selfish individuals. It was my belief that a team might contribute to each other's creative ideas that were discussed in our sales meetings. It was working so far, and I didn't want to change it.

Shortly thereafter, Terry came aboard with an energy and enthusiasm that were contagious. Even Pamela applauded his hire.

"I must admit I was skeptical at first, but I think Terry looks like a good hire," she announced while reviewing her weekly call report in my office. "He's got a lot to learn but has a lot of smarts."

Having Pamela on my side was a big plus since her opinion was valued by the sales team. As a market veteran, she'd seen salespersons come and go and would often share her thoughts with other members of the team. Her positive impression carried a lot of weight.

Terry picked up the basics quickly. We made sales calls on his assigned accounts and worked together to showcase I-95 FM's ratings along with spot packages on the station. Although his billings grew slowly, Terry didn't lose enthusiasm for the station and his chances to grow and prosper.

On more than one occasion, he arrived in my office with ideas on how he might sell a difficult client. His technique was not unique—it stemmed from an ability to get to know clients quickly and become friends to most. It did, however, require nights out entertaining potential clients, especially of the female variety. My attempts at warning him that continual use of his hormonal prowess would make working with customers difficult in future dealings, but my suggestion did little to curtail his partying. After all, he was a recent college graduate and I couldn't blame him. In fact, I occasionally spent time with him—with the idea that we might hunt business—at industry parties and the after party when it allowed.

Terry continually observed how Carol Seiss grew her billing with nightclub business, and he was aggressively hunting his own. On one occasion he came to me with an idea for a brand new club that was planning a grand opening in Miami Springs.

"Rick, I have an appointment on Thursday with Brad Stock and his brother Gabe at Club Saturn. It's the first time they've been in the club business, and they are converting a three-level bar and disco. It's going to be the largest club in Miami, and they are large I-95 fans. I've come up with an idea that they'll love and will sell them on a long-term contract."

"What is it?" I asked.

"I need to bring it up at a promotions meeting. But here

it is: Let's say that we dedicate Thursday night "party night" from Club Saturn. During each evening, we'll simulate our on-location presence through 'live' phone call commercials by our own "Dr. Party" from the club. What better way to bring a live sounding on-air party to our listeners and encourage them to join the real party at the Club Saturn?"

"I love it! Let's talk to Monique."

I stood and walked to the office of Monique Cassel, the station's promotions manager. Although she had cut her teeth creating and supporting station promotions, Monique had become a valuable asset to the sales department, for which we were thankful. Monique had developed a cordial relationship with Kenny Leonard, I-95 FM's "wonder-kid" program direc-tor. Although Kenny was steadfast in his policy to keep the sound of the station clean and despised advertiser promo-tions, Monique had become adept at picking and choosing the times and moments to approach him with sales promo-tions. Much of her convincing took place after hours over sushi at a local restaurant. When the sales promotion bene-fited the station first, he was usually okay with running the promotion.

After listening carefully to Terry's idea, I could tell that Monique's wheels were turning. The concept made sense. Tak-ing the station's nighttime party atmosphere out to a club with live spots would be a plus for our listeners and Club Saturn's location. Monique had no doubt that Kenny would go for it and, as it turned out, he did. As long as the live spots were taken from allotted sales inventory, he was okay. All that was left was for Terry and me to pitch the idea to the client.

Miami Springs is a small town that borders the Miami air-port. Terry had made an appointment there with one of the Club Saturn owners—the managing brother—on a Monday afternoon. (Monday's were always the best day to call on club owners as they would be flush with weekend cash and open to spending it if they thought it could bring them additional business.)

We arrived for our appointment on time at 3:00 p.m., but were still waiting to see Brad Stock at 3:45 p.m.

"What's with this guy?" I asked Terry. "I've got better things to do than wait to see a nightclub owner."

"He always runs late. He probably has another salesman in his office with him."

At the time, I didn't know that Brad was keeping the salesman in high "spirits" during their meeting and had lost track of time. At 4:00 p.m., Brad's office door opened and, sure enough, a man dressed in shirt and tie with a briefcase emerged. They shook hands and bid each other good-bye.

Brad appeared somewhat disheveled and looked as if he hadn't slept in days. He was wearing a wrinkled short-sleeve shirt open to his navel with a long gold chain with a gold Miami Dolphins logo attached to it. He had several dark circles under his eyes that were indicative of a party lifestyle.

"Terry, how are you?" asked Brad in an unusually animated tone. "Is this your manager?"

"Yes, Brad. I'd like you to meet Rick Charnack."

I reached out to shake Brad's hand, and he responded with a limp, clammy hand. *Ugh!*

"Nice to meet you, Brad," I responded.

Brad had beads of sweat on his forehead and eyes like pinheads.

"So, what do you think of my club? Better yet, let me take you on the tour."

This will be interesting. I hope he doesn't trip and fall all over himself.

"My brother and I leased this location from Gilly's, a chain of liquor stores and dance clubs. We flipped when we saw that each of the three floors had a large bar, tables, and visual access to the giant dance floor on the first level."

We spent the next fifteen minutes moving very quickly up and down the club stairs, listening to Brad's diatribe about how the club was to be the largest and most glamorous in Miami. His blabbing was only interrupted by a constant sniffling as if he had a head cold. At one point, Terry nodded at me as if we both knew the reason he was so charged up.

We ended the tour, returned to the office, and Brad closed the door. He asked us to sit and immediately opened a desk drawer revealing a sandwich-size baggie filled with white powder.

"I hope you don't mind if I have a line or two," he said. *So this is why he looks as if sleep has eluded him for days.*

"No problem," responded Terry.

"Please join me." He emptied a healthy pile of the powder and began to cut it in lines on his desk. "You know, everyone that does business here needs to take part in my refreshments. Here, Terry."

Terry gave me a sheepish grin and leaned over the desk to partake in the "cocktail." He took a straw from Brad that had been cut in half and slowly leaned over the desk and snorted a line.

"There you go," laughed Brad. "Now it's your turn, Rick."

"I'm afraid not," I responded. "I've a meeting with corporate later and don't think it would be a good idea to begin getting high so early." *Ha ha, sure you do! Hope this guy bites on my excuse.*

"Okay, Rick, I'll let you pass this time. But remember, any time you come to my club, you're here to party, business or no business."

"Fine, Brad." *This might be better than I thought.* "Speaking of business, Terry has a phenomenal idea to share with you."

"It better be a good one, Terry. The Hispanic station, 'Jammin Q,' just left here and they're coming back with a proposal. What makes you think that I-95 can deliver some of the Latin customers I'm looking for?"

"Because I-95 can deliver both Anglo *and* Hispanic listeners, Brad," I chimed in. "Why settle for just one or the other when you can have *both?*"

Brad leaned over the table and snorted another line of cocaine loudly. "Okay, how do you intend to bring them both to Club Saturn?"

"It's very simple," said Terry. "You've heard of Dr. Party, our late-night deejay and weekend dance party host, right?"

"Think so," nodded Brad, his eyelids now drooping more by the second.

"Well," continued Terry, "we're going to have him do guest appearances at the club and live call-in spots, twice each hour. It will sound as if I-95 is partying at your club!" Brad extended the straw to Terry who snorted another line, as if he were punctuating the sentence.

"Hold on a minute," commented Brad, as he picked up the phone. He peered at it as if his eyesight was impaired and punched several numbers on it. Apparently, the phone rang several times as Brad thumbed his desk with a Latin drumbeat. "Hey, Gabe, come down here for a moment. I want you to listen to this."

Brad's older brother Gabe was really the top decision maker. Terry had filled me in during our drive to the club that we'd have to sell both on the idea, and he was right. It was a good sign that Brad had called Gabe and we would be sitting with both momentarily. In a matter of minutes, Gabe appeared in the doorway.

"Hey, brother, what's up?" he asked.

"These guys are from I-95 and want to bring the station here on Thursday nights and go live."

"Wait a moment," chimed in Terry. "That's not what I said. We want to bring one of our deejays, Dr. Party, to the club on Thursday nights to emcee the fun and call in two live spots on the air each hour that he's here. It will sound like a live station party from Club Saturn."

"You think that will work?" asked Gabe, with a smirk on his face.

"If you run enough advertising on the station each week *along* with the live spots, it will," Terry responded.

Brad, finishing up another snort, jumped in. "How much is enough?"

"Spots and appearance fees about $4,000 per week," said Terry.

"You're kidding, right?" asked Brad. "You've been snorting too much of my coke."

"He's not," I said. "Your club is huge. The competition in the area is sparse. You're positioned for a big win, and we now own Dade County. We should be your largest advertising expense."

"With that kind of money, you will be," offered Gabe.

I looked at Terry, who was now tapping his foot wildly from the effects of the cocaine. He spoke up. "We can get started next week. Let's move, Brad and Gabe."

I looked at Gabe's face. He appeared deep in thought. Brad, on the other hand, appeared wrecked, so I assumed that he would be the easy one to close. Gabe tried to lock eyes with him and wasn't able to. He finally spoke. "I'm okay with it if Brad is. Are you, Brad?"

"Uh-huh," groaned Brad as he reached into the desk drawer for his plastic bag of coke.

"Stop snortin' that stuff for a second!" demanded Gabe. "Let's make certain we are making a good deal."

"Sure." Brad looked up from his desk to stare at Terry. "You giving me free promos?"

Terry looked at me, waiting for an answer. Suddenly the room was quiet as all faces now faced me. I realized that programming would not contribute any station promotional announcements and that it would be necessary to find a creative way to add value to a large order.

"Yes," I said. "We'll promote the night by adding an additional ten seconds to several of the commercials you are airing."

"How many?" asked Gabe.

"A minimum of ten each week."

"Make it fifteen, and we've got a deal."

"Let's compromise. How about twelve?"

"Brad, what do you think?"

"I still think I'd like to have the station run no-charge spots. We are going to be the station's largest advertiser, chrissakes!"

"Can't do it, Brad," I countered. "What I can do is offer the spots for fifty dollars apiece, 6:00 a.m. to 6:00 p.m., wherever we might have time available."

"Sure, but how many are really going to run during the day?"

"Brad, if we run a schedule of ten commercials and only five run during the day, you'll be ahead of the game."

"Okay, that sounds more like it. You okay with it brother?" replied Brad.

"It's your move, Brad. If you're okay with it, I say let's go," said Gabe.

Terry was about to jump out of his skin. It was the largest order he had ever written in the radio business.

"Thank you both," exclaimed Terry. "I'm going to make

certain that Club Saturn is famous in Miami." *Sure you are. We've just sold a schedule with an additional ten seconds at no charge!*

"Thanks," I added.

"Now," declared Brad, "let's celebrate with a large line!"

Gabe leaned over the desk and snorted a line. Terry, gazing at me with a look of guilt, leaned over and joined him. When Brad handed me the straw I sensed I needed to seal the deal. *Oh, what the hell!* I leaned over and snorted a line.

Naturally, as in each case where cocaine is involved, one hit was not enough and the celebration continued. The next thing I realized was it was almost 9:00 p.m. *Time to get the hell out of here!*

Terry and Brad were contemplating the meaning of life when I broke into the conversation. "Terry, we've got to go. I've got plans for the evening."

"Right," confirmed Terry. "We'll pick up this conversation next time I'm here, Brad."

"You certain you can't stay?" inquired Brad, as he continued to cut lines of coke on his desk. *What's this guy? A coke dealer?*

"Nope. I've got to get back to the station. But I'll see you in a few days."

I stumbled over the chair as I stood, but steadied myself. My mind was running a million miles per hour and my jaw was beginning to hurt. Both of my nostrils were numb, and my heart was pounding. Terry and I bid our farewell to Brad and Gabe, who had opened the office door and walked out ahead of us and into the club. The club was beginning to fill up, and I could hear Eddy Grant's "Electric Avenue" playing in the background. Terry was eyeing the club patrons and about to cruise the bar for single girls. I motioned to him to catch up, as I wanted out as soon as possible. I bid Gabe a farewell and thanked him for the order. Terry followed suit.

When we left the club and arrived at my car, I turned to him. "Congratulations, Terry. You did a great job and deserved the order and celebration that followed."

When we sat in the car and I started the engine, Terry turned to me. "Would you mind if I cranked up the radio?"

"No problem," I responded as he turned on the radio.

The car was suddenly filled with music broadcasted from I-95 FM: "Let It Whip" by the Dazz Band. I looked over at Terry. He was pumping his arms up in the air while dancing in the car seat. He was elated and on his way to stardom on the rush of nightclub owners who were coke addicts. *And I was enjoying the pleasures of participating while he made it happen!*

Chapter 22

A HOT MONDAY

During the sixties, a strip spanning three miles in northern Miami Beach was developed with two-story motels and affectionately branded as "Motel Row." It was conceived for those not fond of fancy hotels and the high price of staying at one. As real estate became scarce, developers searched for other locations to accommodate the winter influx of travelers.

One developer, however, had a plan to erect a large hotel on the last vacant property and promote it as the final luxury resort on the beach. His palace, the Greek Isle, was designed as an alternative to the dearth of motels and provided "affordable luxury" to sun seekers. It was in close proximity to the community of Green Palms, an exclusive enclave of oceanfront and inland waterway known as the Intracoastal, which ran parallel to the Atlantic Ocean.

At the time, Green Palms had earned a reputation for two things: a police department that often handed out speeding tickets to motorists exceeding an absurd 20 miles per hour speed limit along the stretch of highway A1A that traversed the community, and an anti-Semitic population. A certain sense of irony existed, because Greek Isle's developers were one of Miami's high-profile Jewish families, the Cohens, and many of their hotel rooms overlooked the pricey Green Palms homes.

As a teenager, I recall attending the opening weekend celebration at the Greek Isle. Dwarfing the two-story motels along the strip, its gleaming gold, blue, and green tile façade was a sight to behold. There were lit fountains shooting water high along its lower concourse entrance and Greek music blaring from loudspeakers. Belly dancers filled the lobby.

The Greek Isle was the most glorious hotel north of Miami Beach, and business flourished for more than two decades, until the Bahamas began to attract northern sun worshippers with grander beachfront hotels and gambling. Due to the decline of business and the hotel's aging condition, the Cohens were forced to re-brand the once-grand Greek Isle into a low-cost vacation package alternative for the price-conscious Canadian market, resulting in the hotel's ultimate deterioration.

In a desperate attempt to create cash flow from every available part of his slumping business, Sandy Cohen decided to lease space on the lower-concourse hotel entrance that once housed many fancy retail establishments. One of the more spacious areas had once featured a discotheque that was shut down when tourism fell off.

Sandy reached out to several club owners, none of whom envisioned customers traveling forty-five minutes to "Motel Row" to party, since there were other clubs much closer to the Miami and Fort Lauderdale populations. Luckily, he finally hit on a business entrepreneur who hungered to chase his dream of becoming a club owner. Sandy eventually worked out a lease to Stuart Pavalo, the said entrepreneur. Stuart had a vision for the club and recognized the importance of consistent advertising to draw crowds to his new disco.

Enter I-95 FM's veteran account executive, Pamela Stein. Pam had built a reputation as a client-focused seller with amazing candor, which advertisers found in meager supply with Miami radio salespersons. Among the many stations that were asked to send a salesperson to the club to pitch for the business, it was I-95 FM's Pam whose honest style appealed to Stuart, and he awarded Pam 100 percent of the radio budget for his Club Caribbean.

"We've got Club Caribbean!" Pam grinned, walking into my office. "They're giving us 100 percent of their budget! I sold them Wednesday-night parties with Johnny Starr!"

An excited Pam quickly turned and left my office to iron out the details with our promotions team.

In a very short time, Johnny was doing his thing at Club Caribbean. Word had spread that it was worth the trip to Motel Row, and the club quickly established a draw from long distances in Miami and Fort Lauderdale. Stuart Pavalo had found his recipe for success. It was the right time, right place, and right advertising choice: I-95 FM.

Because of his close business relationship with Pam and despite the station's policy to collect payment in advance for clubs' advertising schedules, Pam persuaded me to allow Stuart to pay for his schedules each Monday from his weekend receipts. Pam would drive to Club Caribbean on Monday to receive payment, in cash, for his previous week's schedule. He would place the cash in a brown paper bag for Pam. (It became a habit that many nightclub advertisers paid with brown paper bags filled with cash.) These large payments were always the source of jokes from everyone at the station. *Did someone just hold up a bank?*

Meanwhile, Stuart's business had grown steadily and his cash flow was so strong that when Club Caribbean's lease came up for renewal, Sandy Cohen, realizing that his property was reaping big profits, opted to hike Stuart's rent to an unreasonable level. An annoyed Stuart began searching for a larger location to expand his business. *He had bailed Sandy out! What does he expect? Higher rent for the same dump?*

On one of his scouting excursions, Stuart came upon a restaurant in North Miami that would be his ticket to even greater fortune—and fame—in the nightclub business. In fact, because of his close relationship at the time, and as someone he liked and helped build his business through creative promotions, he contacted Pam and arranged to meet her at the potential site. *I wondered, what's really going on with Pam and Stuart?* She also knew that the move to a larger spot would warrant an increase in Stuart's advertising budget, so it was a win–win for all parties.

Following his inspection of a now-defunct restaurant and positive input from Pam, Stuart made a decision to sign a long-term lease. As part of the lease, he would completely renovate the restaurant with an expenditure close to one million dollars for the new Club Caribbean. The club would "have it all" and replicate a *Miami Vice* ambience—modern lines including white sofas, blue and overhead strobe lighting, transparent bars, open ceilings with sparkling star lights, and a small speedboat in the entrance area.

Opening night was an extravaganza.

"I'm speechless!" Pam shrieked. "The parking lot is overflowing with cars, and I noticed several newspaper writers!"

"It's a dream come true," responded Stuart. "Look at this crowd! This is truly my baby!"

Nattily dressed customers were waiting outside in a line surrounding the building: men in pastel suits and women in tight dresses and stiletto high heels. *Don Johnson look-a-likes everywhere!*

Inside the club, drinks were flowing. Michael Jackson's "Billy Jean" had customers packed on Club Caribbean's huge dance floor. Stuart had spared no expense when constructing the sound system and placing giant six-foot-tall bass speakers surrounding the dance floor. Several intoxicated patrons had opted to climb up on the speakers and were dancing amid a faux smoke-filled room. White lights shone out through the smoke clouds in unison with the music.

The club was an instant hit. Weekend crowds replicated the grand opening scenario. Pam pushed for larger schedules. *More cash in the brown paper bags!*

Within a year, under the watchful eye of an exceptional I-95 salesperson and stellar promotional campaigns, Stuart had reached the pinnacle of success in a very competitive nightclub business.

However, six months following the first-year anniversary, business started falling off. Apparently, Club Caribbean had fallen out of fashion. Call it a fickle market. Call it the fact that big spenders are moving targets attracted to anything new. Whatever the reason, the luster was finally off the diamond, and Club Caribbean was in a tailspin.

What did Stuart do? He did what any ego-inflated owner would. He summoned his favorite advertising salesperson and her station promotions manager to the club to provide a rescue scheme. They both arrived at the club on a Monday following an awful weekend of business.

"Stuart, I'd like you to meet Monique, I-95's promotions manager," said Pam. "She's got a great idea for you to bring business back on Friday nights."

Following her introduction, Monique went into a dog-and-pony show about how she had hit on an exciting angle. All Club Caribbean commercials for the upcoming four weeks would include information about a dance contest with a progressive prize giveaway. First week might be tickets to a comedy club. Second week was a gift certificate to one of Miami's famous trendy restaurants. Third was a weekend stay at a local hotel. And, finally, a grand prize: an all-expenses paid trip to Cancun, Mexico.

"What do I need to spend to pull this together?" asked Stuart.

"Just stay with your current schedule," responded Pam as Monique kicked her under the table. *What? Why would you be giving so much to a client without asking for more schedule money?*

When Monique came back to the station and told me of the developments, I almost fell out of my chair. It was an all or nothing-at-all challenge, and I didn't like the odds. And, I thought about penalizing Pam by removing a current billing account from her list because she failed to make the deal predicated on adding more commercials to Stuart's schedule.

What added insult to injury is that the promotion never attracted the large crowd that had been promised. Friday night business improved just slightly at Club Caribbean. What was once a standing-room-only, hot, dance club had—unfortunately—turned into an also-ran destination.

Pam gallantly did her best to assuage Stuart's declining confidence in the club. On the final Friday night of the contest, Pam brought her husband, Richard, to the club. They danced and partied all night along with a sparse crowd until closing time.

There was little more Pam could do. The promotion had flopped, and Stuart's hopes of bringing back Club Caribbean's glory days were dashed. As she was ready to leave, Stuart offered to make payment for the advertising so she wouldn't have to make a return trip on Monday.

"Let me pay you for this week's schedule," Stuart offered.

"Don't worry!" responded Pam, feeling no pain from the alcohol she had imbibed. "Richard and I are having such a great time, so I'd like to keep business separate from pleasure."

"But it will save you a trip on Monday."

"You know how much I enjoy our Monday get-togethers. And, besides, we should probably decide where we go from here." *Go from here? The place is bleeding red ink, and we want to add more to the deficits?*

As sales manager, I would kick off each week by holding a sales meeting on Monday morning. On the Monday following the Club Caribbean debacle, Pam arrived at the meeting in a state of despair, the likes of which I had never seen. She was crying hysterically, could barely speak, and when I saw her walk into the office, I opted to call off the sales meeting and speak with her in the privacy of my office.

"Have you been listening to the news this morning?" she said through her tears.

"No," I responded. "Why?"

"Then you haven't heard about the fire in North Miami that's consuming my largest account, Club Caribbean!" *Oh no, it's our station's largest account, too!*

"We've got to go see Stuart. I need to find out what happened!" cried Pam.

I believed in supporting my salespersons, especially in a situation like this. It was second nature, particularly since she and Stuart had built such a close relationship. That's what made Pam so good. She really *cared* about her customers. We dashed out of the radio station and drove to the club.

Upon our arrival, we witnessed the total devastation of the fire. The building had literally burned to the ground, and only a shell of steel girders, the large Club Caribbean sign, and steadily rising smoke and ashes remained. Several fire trucks were on the scene, continuing to douse water on the smoldering remains. A television van was parked in the parking lot with its broadcast "tower" raised in the air. In addition, a news helicopter hovered over what remained of the building.

We noticed Stuart, safe and sitting on the hood of his red Mercedes Benz outside of the yellow tape that surrounded the property at the edge of the parking lot. He saw us approaching.

"Stuart!" cried Pam. "What happened?"

"It's gone. My baby's gone!"

"What happened?"

"I had just left the club and drove up the street to get coffee. As I drove past the club to head home, I saw smoke. And now it's gone."

"Oh my God, this is horrible. What are you going to do?" asked Pam.

"Thank God, I'm insured. I'm going to find out what happened here and then contact my insurance agent."

Pam turned to me, her eyes swelling with tears.

"Can we stay with Stuart for a while?"

"Sure, but I have an appointment at the station at 10 a.m."

"Why don't you go on," said Stuart. "There's nothing much you or I can do here."

"I really feel like staying here with you, Stuart. We've been through so much together! *What does that mean?* Are you certain?" implored Pam.

"Absolutely."

Even though he was in a state of shock, Stuart apologized to Pam because he wouldn't be able to pay for his advertising. Stuart also mentioned something about having wanted to give her money on Friday night and how she should have accepted it before she and Richard left the club.

On the way back to the station, I turned to Pam and asked her what Stuart meant about the money and Friday night. She told me that she and Richard were having so much fun partying she had refused to take the brown bag, opting to wait until Monday.

"What?" I blurted out. "He offered you money, and you refused it!" *Please . . . tell me this isn't so!*

"It's true. I never thought anything like this could happen but wouldn't be surprised if the fire wasn't an 'accident.'"

"You know your customer far better than I do. What are you saying?"

"I'm saying that he's been piling up financial losses since the club went downhill."

"And, knowing this, you didn't take his money when you were at the club?"

"Okay, blame me. We were really having fun on Friday night."

"Fine. Just come up with a plan to replace the dollars you will lose from this account no longer advertising on the station."

Pam began sobbing. "I'm sorry!" *You're sorry. I'm about to eat the entire week's worth of advertising and lose a major account!*

I tried to understand what had just happened, the absurdity of Pam turning down payment from an advertiser, and the advertiser losing his business to a fire. The irony was too much.

I turned to Pam. "Well, I hope you enjoyed dancing your ass off," I said.

"It was the most expensive dancing I've ever done," responded Pam.

"And it was the most costly brown bag you neglected to pick up!" I added.

My thoughts turned to a similar incident when I was a salesperson making my weekly sales call at a club. When I arrived, I found a large padlock on the front door and a police poster that revealed the club had been closed due to nonpayment of rent. *Oh, the travails of calling on nightclubs!*

As I conveyed the story to Pam, she turned to me with teary eyes. "What am I going to do about the billing?" she asked.

"You'll make it up somehow, Pam." I replied.

"Where?"

"Well, there's always a new nightclub opening in South Florida."

"I know. That's what concerns me."

"Do you want me to assign nightclub leads to someone else?"

"Not a chance."

"Fine. But this time make certain you collect your money before you dance."

I looked over to Pam and noticed she had stopped sobbing. We both broke into roaring laughter. Failure to collect a client's money. Her largest account gone up in flames. A client trying to console himself by thinking only of his insurance policy. All made for a very ironic episode.

And, yes, it was another example of Murphy's Law at its best. A salesperson "trusting" an advertiser. A nightclub going up in flames. A bagful of money lost. *Just another nightclub story from the eighties!*

Chapter 23

NEW BUSINESS CONSULTANT

Following a successful two-year run of nightclub business, Carol Seiss, my top local biller, was no longer satisfied with chasing retail business and dance club owners. Her constant attendance at weekend promotions was burning her out, so she was eager for a new challenge and had more than once suggested she could help the team develop new dollars on the station.

As there were no obvious management jobs available, I decided to make a new position available to keep her in the company.

Since Carol specialized in creating new business that had yielded her big orders, it made sense to create a business development manager position for her so that she might help other sellers do the same. The station manager, Syd Stone, was all for a promotion, and working out the details were easy. Carol was to continue working with several of her current accounts at first and also help the sales teams develop fresh retail dollars. She was to receive a stipend for each new account, and eventually I'd reassign her accounts to other salespersons.

Shortly after receiving the promotion, Carol appeared in my office.

"Rick, I've been doing some research. I propose that we hire a consultant to help me and our staff learn the ins and outs of developing fresh dollars."

"What do you have in mind?"

"In my research, I've discovered a consultant from Chicago who I have high regard for. Her name is Sherry Chastain, and she specializes in working with salespersons and business development managers in the pursuit of new retail business. I've spoken with her on numerous occasions and like the training materials she sent me. Frankly, Rick, it will be a critical component to making my new department successful."

Carol placed a red binder on my desk, turned it around, and showed me examples of Sherry's approach to developing new dollars and several examples of successful promotions that were aired on stations with which Sherry worked.

"Here's an example promotion that yielded fifteen thousand dollars. One of the sales reps at a station she consults works with Mainline Grocery Stores. Her idea was to place a small sailboat at the end of a supermarket aisle filled with various grocery items. Sherry was able to tap into some of the stores' allocated co-op dollars.

"That's clever. I like the sound of fifteen thousand!"

"I could never do something like that on my own. I need training if we are going to make something of this department."

"I know that this will come with a cost. What are we talking about?"

"An up-front charge of five thousand dollars for training me and the sales teams, a monthly retainer of five hundred dollars, and travel expenses."

"That's eleven thousand dollars I haven't set aside in this

year's budget, Carol. My entire training budget for the year is approximately three thousand dollars, which is eight thousand dollars less than what you need!"

"Our first sale should cover it."

"It doesn't work that way. I'll have to get Syd to play with the numbers and find the money. I'm behind you and the station believes in you, so let me see what I can do."

"Then when can you have this approved?"

"Give me a few days."

"Rick, I need to get back to Sherry. She's on a tight schedule, and if we're going to get started in the next thirty days, I need to commit to her by next Tuesday."

"What? Why the rush?" *She's now using her talent for closing deals on me! No wonder she's successful!*

"The only rush is my need to get started, Rick. I think I can arrange to have Sherry come here within the next thirty days."

"So you've really done your research? You're fully satisfied that there's no one else out there who can provide you with the type of training you need?"

"Not unless we can spend upward of twenty thousand dollars!"

"The money's important, but so is the quality of training."

"I've spoken with Sherry a number of times, and we have a great connection. I'm confident she's our best bet."

"Okay, let's see if I can get the money appropriated."

The following day I met with Syd. I told him that in order to confidently move forward with Carol we needed to provide the training support she was asking for. He hemmed and hawed about the money, but with a little bit of arm-twisting—moving dollars from one budget line to another—Syd eventually came around. If the stations were to move ahead with the development of new dollars and make good on a new department, our newly appointed manager needed proper training. As soon as I had his approval, I told an excited Carol.

"You won't be disappointed, Rick."

"Make me proud, that's all."

Carol and Sherry made arrangements to have I-95's sales department available for full-day training sessions on a date within the next few weeks. At the appointed date, Sherry arrived at the station ready to train. Carol escorted her into my office.

"Rick, I'd like you to meet Sherry Chastain," she said.

Sherry bent over my desk and shook my hand. She smiled at me and, for the first time, I could see why Carol admired her. She was petite, just over five feet tall, with pixie-styled brown hair that reminded me of a character in a children's book. She was wearing a green turtleneck sweater that was going to be far too hot in the Florida weather, and matching plaid slacks. Her wide-smile lips were punctuated with bright red lipstick. What she lacked in physical stature, she apparently made up for with her presence and bubbly personality.

"Great to meet you, Rick," she offered. "I'm pleased that we could put an agreement together. In speaking with Carol a number of times, I have reason to believe that she has the stuff to be one of my best students. Are you holding a sales meeting to introduce me to your staff?"

"Work out the details with Carol, and let me know what works best."

"Okay, I'm ready to get started."

Carol leaned over my desk. "I suggest that we gather in the conference room as soon as possible."

"Fine."

Carol and Sherry quickly set up a schedule of training

meetings with I-95 FM's sales team. She brought bright red binders for each of the sellers and spent the next several days in meetings presenting the basics of developing new business through promotions and the use of co-op dollars. I was pleasantly surprised about how eager some of the salespersons were to join forces with Carol. There were others who resented Carol's assent to a management position; she was so laser focused it was scary. But as long as there was enough activity on the business development front, I reasoned that we could justify the expense.

Following the first day of training, I was feeling confident that Carol had found the right person to help her. She and Sherry shared their enthusiasm with me in my office.

"Amazing staff, Rick!" exclaimed Sherry. "This team is soaking up the information and is eager to get started!"

"Better yet," I countered, "let's start making sales calls. Always best to take advantage of the positive energy."

"Perhaps we can schedule a few calls this afternoon," offered Carol.

"Set up your calls and go for it," I said. They both left my office, and I assumed it was to touch base with any number of salespersons.

Following an afternoon of fact-finding with salespersons at several retail accounts, I received word from Carol that her first day had been successful. I was optimistic and immediately conveyed my confidence in the program to Syd. He was enthusiastic but tempered it with a reminder of the large investment the station was making. *Burst my balloon, why don't you?*

On the morning of her second day of training, Sherry showed up, walked into my office, and appeared hunched over.

"Are you okay?" I asked.

"Not really. I have a bad back and must have slept in an awkward position. I'm in a lot of pain."

Benji Weinstein, a salesperson always up for a practical joke, was in earshot of Sherry and entered my office.

"I've just the thing to fix you up." Benji walked out of my office and quickly returned with a white pill in his hand.

"Take this. It will fix you right up."

"What is it?"

"It's medication that I take for my back."

"Are you sure? I don't want to space out during the meetings."

"You won't," Benji assured. "I take them all the time."

Sherry left my office, presumably headed to the water fountain to take the pill. With a wry look on his face, Benji spoke: "Wait until you see what happens to her."

"What on earth did you give her?" I asked Benji.

"A Quaalude."

"Are you kidding? She's here for training, on my dime. She's going to be wrecked!"

"That's the point."

"Are you nuts? I'm all for practical jokes, Benji, but with this one you've gone way over the top!"

"Don't worry. She'll be fine."

"Oh thanks." *There goes a day of training down the drain!*

I hated to admit, however, that I was amused. Benji and I had teamed up on numerous station and client pranks. His market reputation was well known, and he was hilarious.

Sherry reappeared and invited us to join her in the conference room. It didn't take long for the medication to take effect. Soon after reviewing the prior day's material, Sherry seemed confused.

"Open your binder to the second section—or is it the third? No matter. Let's start with the third." She began swaying to the left and right as if there were music playing in the background. The salespersons in attendance were startled.

After all, they had come to respect Sherry as an expert, and Carol had assured them that her hiring would take them to the "promised land" of new business.

Carol looked at me and motioned toward the door. She whispered in my ear, "May I speak with you for a moment?"

I escorted Carol out of the conference room and closed the door behind her.

"What's going on with Sherry?" she asked. "She looks high."

"Well," I responded, "Benji gave her some pain medication because she complained of severe back pain."

"What did he give her?"

"A Quaalude, I think."

"What? Are you crazy?"

"She'll be fine. Let's get back into the meeting."

We returned to the conference room to hear Sherry say, "Open your binders, ha ha . . ." The room became silent.

"C'mon," begged Sherry, as she began to circle the conference table. "I'm ready to begin the training and am feeling great. Is there any music in here? I'm ready to dance. Anyone want to dance?"

Sherry then raised her arms in front of the room as if she were at a disco. I gazed over at Benji who was hiding his face behind a legal pad. Carol was frozen with a stunned look on her face.

"Mmm, mmm," groaned Sherry, tiptoeing across the front of the conference room. "Super freak, super freak, that girl's a super freak, ohh!" *She's whacked! What's next? A contest emceed by the consultant?*

"It appears that you are ready to party, Sherry," I countered. "Let's take a break. Carol will let you know when we'll reconvene."

The room emptied while Sherry continued to pirouette in front of the room.

"No, Rick, the party's just getting started! On second thought, I think I'll sit down" she said, letting out a sigh and taking a seat in one of the conference room chairs.

Carol took a seat on the opposite side of the conference table. I turned to Sherry. "You're going to need to get it together."

"What do you mean by 'together,' Rick? My back feels great!"

I looked across the table at Carol, who now appeared shell-shocked.

"What do you want to do, Carol?" I queried.

"Sherry, you're unable to train today," said Carol. "Clearly we cannot go on sales calls!"

"I'm fine. Anyone know where I can buy some cocaine? It will settle me down." *What the hell? I'm paying her $11,000 for this?*

I had few options. We could continue training, which would be a bad idea considering Sherry's uncertain condition. I decided to have her spend the day reviewing material with Carol. Having her train my salespersons in her condition was too risky. They would undoubtedly lose respect for her and, if Syd happened to check in and see her, it would be a disaster.

I retreated to my office and found Benji inside waiting for me.

"Can you believe her? She's stoned!" offered Benji.

"Sure. You knew what you were getting her into. What did you expect?" I smirked.

"If she's still hurting later, I've got more where that came from."

"Don't bet on it."

Benji stood and left my office. Before leaving he said, "I'm available for dinner if you want to take her out."

Later that day, at 5:30 p.m., Carol appeared at my office door. "Can you take her off of my hands, please?"

I agreed to take Sherry to dinner with Benji. Carol escorted Sherry into my office and said goodnight.

"Hungry?" I asked Sherry.

"Famished!" I haven't had a thing to eat all day, but Carol and I accomplished a great deal."

"How's your back feeling?"

"My back's hurting me again." *Sure. I'm certain Benji will provide more pain relief!*

I decided to take Sherry and Benji to eat stone crab at one of Miami's famous restaurants. When we arrived and were seated, Benji handed us each a white pill. Sherry swallowed hers before the waiter came over. I looked around and took stock of the room. Lots of mostly conservative men were wearing suits, probably a collection of businessmen and lawyers who were there to conduct business. *If they only knew what we were up to!*

It didn't take long before Sherry was snapping her fingers in the air and laughing hysterically. Benji, of course, was encouraging her by sharing in her laughter as if they were trading jokes.

I ordered dinner and a bottle of wine. *Alcohol . . . this can't be a good idea. Oh, what the hell!* The waiter retuned and poured us each a generous glass full of wine. Benji then made a tragic mistake.

To fully illustrate his current state of mind, he reached for a roll and flung it as high as it would go into the air. *Oh, crap now he's done it. Quaaludes and rolls!*

Sherry turned in time to see the roll land squarely on the shoulder of a restaurant patron, one wearing a business suit. It bounced onto the floor next to him. Sherry broke into her now well-known hysterical laughter. I glanced at Benji. He was trying his best to maintain a straight face. I was somewhere in between. Out of the corner of my eye, I could see the maître d' walking toward us. He stopped at our table and addressed the group.

"Are you folks crazy? I'm going to have to ask you to leave if you continue to act like this," he admonished.

"Act like what?" asked Benji.

"Now wait," I said. "If we are guilty of anything, it's enjoying the ambience of your restaurant."

"But our ambience doesn't approve of customers hoisting rolls."

"Okay," I said. "I'm not certain what happened, but we're here to enjoy your stone crab and don't want to cause any problems. We'll keep our frivolity here at our table." *Sure. Easy for me to say.*

We did our best to contain ourselves for the remainder of the meal. After I paid the bill, we stumbled out to the valet who brought our cars. Benji said goodnight and sped off. Sherry fell asleep in my car on the way back to her hotel. When I pulled up to her hotel, she suddenly awakened and, as if nothing had happened, opened her door.

"Want help getting out?" I asked.

"No, I've got it."

She probably won't remember anything that happened. I'm not certain I ever want her to!

Over the next twelve months, Sherry made additional trips to train the teams and develop new business. Unfortunately, her training never achieved the high expectations Carol and I had hoped for. Many involved "pain relief" of one type or another.

We often spent evenings with Benji, Sherry, Terry Webber, Carol, and her fiancé at my apartment playing word games until late into the evening and early morning. Our stimulating conversation was always aided by a variety of mood-altering substances. One time we stayed up way past a reasonable hour, when I suddenly realized that it was a few hours until the business day began. I took Sherry back to her hotel, returned home, and dressed hastily. I drove back to the hotel, picked up Sherry, and arrived at the station in time for our prearranged 8:00 a.m. sales meeting.

"Sherry will be covering important information today," I announced at the head of the conference table. I suggest you listen up because the training might very well involve one of your accounts."

I turned, left the conference room, and headed to my office.

"Hold my calls," I instructed my secretary. "I've some important research to do while the new business training is underway."

"No problem," she replied.

I walked into my office, sat down in my comfortable desk chair, and put my head down on my desk. It seemed only moments later that I heard a knock on my door. I rose and walked over, opening it slowly. It was my secretary, Barbara.

"Carol asked if you could come back to the conference room."

"Sure."

I straightened my tie and walked back to the conference room, opened the door, and the room fell silent. Ten pairs of eyes were staring at me. *What the heck?*

"How's it going?" I asked, looking around the room.

"Great," offered Sherry.

"Terrific!" I responded

"That's a wrap," offered Sherry. "You can go back to your desks. I'll be available to make sales calls with you tomorrow."

"Why not today?" I inquired.

"Because it's five-thirty and everyone's going home."

"Are you serious?"

"Yes," piped up Carol. "What have you been doing in your office all day?"

"Important research," I said.

"You mean, 'important rest' as in sleeping all day," laughed Sherry. *Busted!*

It was true. I had slept the entire day in my office because I hadn't gotten any sleep the night before. It was a first for me. Sleeping all day in my office. Not a good thing. Not a bad thing either as I was totally ready to make plans for another evening out.

Chapter 24

FAST FOOD, ANYONE?

One of my best sellers at I-95 FM, Benji Weinstein, always made going on sales calls with him an adventure. As a senior seller, Benji called on one of the market's largest fast food accounts. Controlling the multimillion-dollar media budget was Betty Larson, a career senior buyer both in age and experience. Betty had relocated from the Midwest and brought a happy hour routine that provided her a daily state of alcoholic bliss.

To conduct business, Betty would accompany her favorite station salespersons for drinks and dinner at an expensive restaurant. At one such event, I was invited to join Benji and Betty at one of her favorite Fort Lauderdale restaurants, The Downunder. And, since the Downunder was one of the priciest in the city, I was also along to pay the check.

The strategy was simple. Hoist enough drinks over dinner and hang in until Betty became inebriated, at which time she would begin the famous cocktail "napkin pass." Betty would propose a rate for the year on a cocktail napkin, pass it to me, and I'd counter with my desired rate and pass it back to her. After several offers and counteroffers, Betty would pass the final offer on a remaining cocktail napkin. After the station approved it, it was a binding contract for the year.

During one of the more memorable evenings, I sat down

for dinner with Betty and Benji at the Downunder. I had told Benji that I was going to be late. By the time I arrived, they were both hoisting down drinks. I was "on the wagon" at the time and noticed two empty glasses, both of which had probably been filled with vodka. I ordered another round for them, and while the waiter sat us down, Benji requested lemons for his drink.

"You want lemonade?" Betty barked at Benji. "Order friggin' lemonade!" Betty roared as Benji and I nodded, knowing that she was well on her way to her notorious stupor.

We ordered dinner and more drinks and, in no time, I noticed that Betty was now leaning in her chair and starting to slur her words. The number of drinks was now affecting Benji, who would punctuate Betty's slurring by kicking me under the table.

During the next fifteen minutes or so, Benji's kicks became more frequent, and had I been intoxicated as he and Betty were, it wouldn't have mattered. However, as my left leg began aching from his numerous kicks, I was inclined to put an end to the madness. With a quick glance at Betty to make certain she wasn't paying attention, I grabbed Benji's shoe and sock, pulling them both from his foot. When he tried to counter with his other foot, I used the same quick motion to remove the other shoe and sock. It didn't matter! He continued to kick me as if he were acting out his drunkenness.

There I was, in a five-star restaurant with a pair of shoes and socks in my lap. In an effort to lighten my load, I placed the socks underneath the breadbasket napkin and summoned a busboy.

"We don't need any more rolls," I said. "You may remove these."

As soon as the rolls were removed with Benji's socks, I turned to Betty.

"Betty, have you ever been to Worth Avenue in Palm Beach?" I asked her.

"Sure. What of it?" she countered, as if she had shopped many of the boutiques along the exclusive avenue.

"It's a very preppy area, right, Betty?"

"Sure, but what's the point?"

"What do you think of highbrow men who wear madras slacks and loafer shoes without socks?

"Who gives a crap?" she retorted, pounding the table. "Where's the waiter? I need a drink!"

A drink? Geez. . . . At this rate of drink consumption, she's going to fall out of her chair.

Obviously, the thought of seeing Benji without socks didn't faze her much. In fact, she couldn't care less.

Shortly after her reply, I felt a crystal-like substance rain onto my lap. Apparently Benji was now tearing sugar packets and heaving the contents under the table in the direction of my lap. *This is far too childish for one of my key salespersons, but I'll wait and see the final outcome of the evening.* These antics continued throughout the dinner and following our napkin negotiation. He fetched items from the table—a fork, lemons from his drinks—and continued throwing them at me. At one point he tried to hurl creamed spinach, but I saw him gathering it on a spoon, and while he was lifting the tablecloth I moved my chair to avoid it. Benji was completely twisted.

When the meal was finished and coffee arrived, I surveyed the table for an item that might be the end game, and my focus came upon a glass of ice water. With a quick glance around the neighboring tables (not that it mattered what they thought anyway), I reached under the table and hurled the glass of water under the table at Benji. *This childishness is now contagious!*

"Oh, my God!" Benji howled as the ice water seared through his slacks.

"What?" slurred Betty. "What is it, my nice Jewish friend?"

"Nothing," responded Benji while bending over the table, his face turning a crimson shade of red.

As punctuation to the ice water, I reached for a small pitcher of cream, brought it under the table, and flung it at him. The effect of ice water and cream ended the match as Benji's surprised look indicated that he had had enough.

I summoned the waiter and requested the check. Both he and Betty were ready to retire—or, better put, expire—from dinner. After I paid the bill, Benji helped Betty out of her chair, steadied her, and began walking toward the exit. They were both too drunk to stand, and he lost his grip on Betty and she fell, knocking a tray table full of dishes to the floor.

"Oh crap!" yelled Betty, to the dismay of the restaurant patrons.

"Don't worry, Betty," offered Benji. "I've got you."

"Hell you don't!" responded Betty. "I've all I can do to drive home."

"I would advise you to allow me to drive you both home," I offered.

"No way!" countered Betty. "I've never allowed anyone to do that!"

"Okay, Betty, then let me help you to your car," I offered.

When her car arrived, I carefully walked her to it. I had my hands full trying to assist her, and the valet was grinning as Betty continued her swearing. Quite remarkably, Betty drove off in a steady direction and left the parking lot.

Benji, on the other hand, stood helplessly at the entrance to the restaurant, the front of his suit jacket and slacks stuck to his body with white blotches covering both in tie-dye fashion. I walked over to help him retrieve his valet ticket. As he handed it to me, we both had a hearty laugh.

"Are you okay, Benji?" I asked. "You look like you've been to hell and back."

"I really don't give a crap," retorted Benji, "as long as I got the deal!"

Chapter 25

THE SPOT GROUP

Throughout my radio career, I've learned that there are advertising agencies that typically stand out as the toughest to do business with. Such was the case with The Spot Group, the largest radio agency in Miami.

Among The Spot Group's employees were two very savvy entrepreneurs who created a following with retailers and automotive dealers because of their expertise in creating successful radio campaigns in South Florida. The campaigns revolved around commercials that were hard hitting, often voiced by someone who sounded like a military sergeant rather than a radio announcer. You had to love the way The Spot Group was using radio, but hate the sound of their abrasive commercials.

Station program directors weren't big fans of running The Spot Group commercials because they were an instant turnoff and might prompt listeners to immediately change the station. However, the dollars being spent by such an agency typically outweighed the latter, and most stations overlooked their bombastic sound.

I had assigned The Spot Group account to a relative rookie in the business, Elena Diaz, an attractive young girl in her mid-twenties. Elena was a "looker"—dark complexion, long brown hair, sexy figure, and a wonderfully exuberant personality. She typically dressed in tight, revealing dresses and heels, and turned heads wherever she went.

When I assigned Elena to call on The Spot Group, I postulated that Scott Sands, the media buyer, might not be able to turn down such a sexy ad rep. Scott was known to appreciate young, hot-looking girls. He had already flirted with Elena but never gave her the time of day when it came to doing business. He took great pride in objectifying women and bashing stations that he didn't do business with. Elena realized she needed thick skin to work with him and managed to hold her own whenever calling on the agency. She knew what was at stake: huge orders and a piece of the budget from our largest competitor, Y100.

Call it fate, or just persistence, but Elena was finally able to convince Scott to consider using I-95 FM for one of his clients. His ego required that sales managers visit the agency to work out a special rate deal.

"I think Scott's ready to buy!" exclaimed Elena with a wide grin as she stepped into my office. "He wants to see you to work out a deal."

"That's great news! Make an appointment, and we'll go see him," I responded.

Great! This is a chance to bring aboard one of the market's largest advertising agencies and the clients it represents.

"What should we charge him?"

"What days and times does he want to buy?"

"You know, Rick, that he only wants to load up during drive times on Wednesday, Thursday, and Friday, our most in-demand time periods. He'll want to buy commercials for one-half of what we charge other advertisers."

"I know. That's why I've always hesitated doing business with The Spot Group. But maybe it's time to evaluate what he can bring to the table. Besides, you've worked hard to get us to the point of being taken seriously."

"Thanks, Rick. I'd be happy to use The Spot Group as an example of how I-95 FM is making strides with important advertisers in the market."

I had my reservations about doing business with Scott. His appalling style of negotiation was a challenge, as he demanded rate discounts that were practically impossible to live with. I recognized the difficulty of doing business with him but wanted to continue to increase the station billing.

Elena set an appointment, and we drove to The Spot Group offices for our meeting at 12:00 p.m. Upon our arrival at the small building in North Miami, we were escorted to a tiny office where Scott was eating lunch at his desk; not like the spacious conference rooms we were accustomed to during a serious rate negotiation, but a room reeking from onions that were apparently a part of his sub sandwich. He motioned to Elena to close the door, and we could barely sit in front of his desk, my knees slamming up against it. *He was clearly trapping us in his small office to gain a psychological advantage.*

We were barely seated when Scott blurted out, "I'm not buying your station. Your ratings suck!"

"C'mon, Scott, you told me to bring my sales manager because you were interested in working out a deal with us," responded Elena.

"I've changed my mind," he responded. "I've looked at the ratings, and Y100 kicks your ass. I've got the market covered with a hefty schedule on them." *Okay, first volley. Time to return his serve.* Scott took a bite of his nasty-smelling sub.

"Okay, let's begin with some facts, Scott," I said. "Y100's audience in Dade County has been eroding with adults, ages eighteen to forty-nine, since we went on the air. We grew in that category by over thirty percent in the last ratings." *I postulated that this was a strong return of his first serve.*

Scott blurted out with a mouth full of sandwich, "But you still haven't as large an audience as they do, and I'm not buying you, ratings increase or not. If I was going to do it, I'd rather work with Elena, Rick. I don't like managers." *I see. He's trying his "insult the manager" trick. Nice try, Scott, I'm not buying this tactic.*

I said, "I thought you wanted me to come with Elena."

"Now that I've met you, Rick, I've changed my mind," he said as he took another bite of his sandwich. *I'm finding it hard to breathe from the onions.*

"Scott, it doesn't matter how you feel about me," I said. "The fact is that it won't be long before I-95 is a major factor in Dade County. Our ratings continue to grow, our programming is perfect for the tri-cultural market, and we have the right promotions in place. If I were to give you a ground-floor deal to get you started on the station, would that change your mind?"

"Maybe, Rick, but it would have to be an amazing deal." *Great. Here's our shot!*

"Let's look at a sample schedule."

I asked Elena to pull out an I-95 FM schedule form from her briefcase. She handed it to me, and I leaned over Scott's desk. First, I showed him where his morning and afternoon drive commercials would air on Wednesday, Thursday, and Friday. I then added Saturday daytime ads. Finally, I completed the schedule by scheduling commercials during the evening and on Sunday. We both looked down on the paper and counted the total commercials: twenty-two.

"That's about right," said Scott.

"Sure, but now let's figure out the cost."

Elena handed me her calculator. I'm going to charge you the lowest drive-time rate on the station and a minimal charge for the other spots. Let's see—the unit rate average for the package is eighty-three dollars!"

"What? Are you kidding?" shouted Scott. "I'm buying Y100 for sixty dollars! You guys aren't worth more than fifty dollars. If you can't give me a fifty-dollar rate, you can kiss my ass!"

"Scott, how many overnights are they giving you to make the deal look good?"

"That's always part of the deal. I demand them. But my deal on Y100 is sixty dollars for *drive-time* spots.

"So you're ready to make a deal at fifty dollars, Scott?"

"Perhaps. But you need to run the schedule that you showed me."

I looked down at the schedule and did some quick calculations in my head. I'd have to practically give away the other spots to make the deal."

"How many advertisers will you be running each week?" I questioned.

Scott turned to Elena. "She already knows that I run at least two per week. At fifty dollars per spot that would be eight thousand dollars each month, or a hundred-and-five thousand dollars for the year. How many other customers are airing over a hundred thousand dollars of business each year on the station?"

"Not many," I responded.

"Then the offer stands," said Scott. He turned to Elena and asked me, "Do you want to stand in the way of Elena's commission because you have no balls, Rick?"

I looked at Scott and said, "I think there's only one person in this transaction who has balls, Scott, and it's you for asking for a fifty dollar rate on I-95!"

"Screw you, Rick," he said.

"Tell you what, Scott. We're close. Your commitment to the station and our growth would be a big win for us both. I'm not looking for the same deal as Y100 now, but I need to get closer to where they are. When I beat their Miami ratings, can you justify increasing our rate?"

"Nice try, Rick. I won't make any promises."

"No promises? I need an option here, Scott. I'm breaking all of my rate rules."

"But I'm probably offering you more money than any other agency in the market."

"True, but not for long. I'm working out deals with soft drink advertisers with much higher rates and year-long contracts."

"Look, Rick, you came here to see me. I didn't want to use your station, but I've a thing for Elena and she's deserving of the business." *A thing? What does that mean?*

"That's honorable, Scott. But this needs to be a business decision. Tell you what. I'll give you the fifty dollar rate for six months but want a minimum increase of ten dollars if our ratings increase at least ten percent with Miami adults eighteen to forty-nine in the fall book."

Scott took a final bite of his sandwich. I could sense he was mulling over the option.

"Scott," encouraged Elena, "it's a great deal."

Hmm. If I make this deal I'll be bringing in the largest order ever written on the station. And we might shoot Y100 in the foot. Those were my goals for coming here in the first place.

Scott added, "You do know I don't accept make-good spots. Anything that doesn't run can't be rescheduled and won't be paid for."

"I'll keep an eye on your schedules," assured Elena.

"So, Rick, it's your decision," confirmed Scott.

"I want a ninety-day evaluation of our agreement, Scott," I responded. "I want the option to renegotiate based on our ratings, demand, and how we are airing your schedules. It's a win-win. You'll only be paying if we deliver a larger audience." *I-95 FM hasn't reached one-half of its potential, and it's a no-brainer for me.*

"Okay," said Scott. "But you better run my schedules as ordered!"

"Fine, let's get it done," I responded.

We shook hands and Scott barked, "Now get out of here. I've got a client meeting in an hour." *Finally! I could have expired from the smell in this room!*

On the way back to the station, we stopped for lunch and a drink. Naturally, Elena was sky high from her largest sale ever. I was happy for her and excited about The Spot Group billing. It was both the largest account in the market and sale on the station.

And the abuse from Scott, not to mention the toxic smell of onions, had been worth it.

Chapter 26

TRIPS AHOY!

Sometimes all that's necessary to earn a large radio order is to offer the client a commercial rate that meets their cost demands. Sometimes it's not enough, and additional incentives are necessary, such as promotions and value added (sponsorships, promotional inventory, or paid travel). Such was the case in selling to a beer distributor's marketing director, Barry Richmond.

Barry loved his job, passing out media dollars in return for a great rate on the station and travel incentives. It was merchandising that bordered on outright bribery, but station managers recognized that in order to do business with him it was necessary to provide "gifts." We often joked about his technique, which also included dealing directly with the station sales management. Although I spent time negotiating the business, I made the account assignment to Terry Webber, one of my account executives, to oversee the preparation of our case for the business, as well as to manage a variety of station promotions that were necessary after securing the deal.

Terry came into my office with the request to negotiate the deal on the phone.

"It's that time, Rick. Barry has requested our response to his annual buy demands. Let's give him a call," said Terry, taking a seat.

I stood, walked to my office door, and closed it so we might have some privacy.

"Is he expecting our call?" I responded.

"Yes."

"What research have you done to earn the business?"

"I've tracked the growth of our audience in the demographic that he buys, and we have a great story. Here are some bullet points that you can read to him during the call."

I looked over the research and admired the thorough job that Terry had done collecting convincing evidence of our growth. It was essential to earning an order from as large an advertiser as Barry represented. We both knew that we only had one shot to earn an annual contract for the business.

"Let's get him on the phone," I said.

I leaned over Terry's notes to retrieve Barry's direct line. I called and enabled the speakerphone so that all of us might hear the conversation. He immediately answered the line.

"Barry Richmond."

"Hi, Barry, it's Rick Charnack and Terry Webber at WINZ-FM, I-95, in Miami. I have you on the speaker so that we can both be part of our conversation."

"Hey, Rick, Terry," answered Barry. "What have you got for me?"

Terry spoke up. "Barry, this is our pitch for an annual order. We feel that our ratings growth in the market has earned us a portion of your budget this year."

"Why is that?" responded Barry.

I started to use the bullet point analysis that Terry had prepared but was immediately interrupted.

"Rick," said Barry, "I have a problem with your station in that your audience is composed of over fifty percent teens. I'm not about to spend booze dollars on a station with a reach composed of a market that I can't use. In fact, our company dictates that we don't buy stations that promote liquor to the teenage market." *He's right. Now what?*

I looked at Terry and motioned for him to counter the argument.

"Barry," said Terry, "the overall station weekly reach might be high in teens, but there are day parts that are less than fifty percent teens and efficient in reaching your target."

It was a great positioning only if Barry's scheduling would allow for the station to air his commercials in time slots that weren't highly rated with teenagers.

"If you're telling me that I need to restrict my schedules to time slots other than what my formula is, I'm not going to do it!" said Barry. *Oh crap! That didn't go well.*

"Look at it this way," answered Terry. "We have personalities that Miami's crazy about, so we can reach your target in their time slots. If we air your schedules during their shows and run promotions involving them, isn't that what you want?"

"You guys aren't listening," countered Barry. "I'm only interested in the big picture. No half-baked rated station."

"Okay," I interrupted, "I get it, Barry." *Let's see if he buys this.* "How would you feel about us running monthly promotions during our afternoon drive-home slot? Our teen composition is less than thirty percent then! We can build appearances that include our most sought-after personality. He's pulling in major ratings."

"I'm not certain that I can justify it, Rick. Remember what I told you about buying stations that offer a high teen audience? It's definitely going against you."

"Barry," I offered, "by passing on I-95 FM as part of your buy, you're eliminating a radio powerhouse in the tenth-largest market in the country. You've got enough dollars to cherry-pick your target. Let me show you how to take advantage of our audience."

"Explain it to me, Rick, and tell me what dollars you are proposing," suggested Barry.

"Terry, what have you got worked up?" I asked.

Terry leaned over toward my phone and its speaker and said, "I'd suggest heavying up your schedule during our promotional weeks—once per month—and running maintenance schedules the remaining weeks. The total monthly frequency would be sixty commercials at a rate of one hundred dollars each.

"I see," answered Barry. "But that rate is way out of line."

"It's fifty percent lower than we're charging . . . you're running commercials during our highest-rated part of the day!" I countered.

"How can you make the deal more attractive, Rick. I'd be going out on a limb for your station."

"I can air commercials that air overnight. Teen listening is very low, and our nightclub audience is very large. I'll give you ten per week at ten dollars each."

"Are you kidding?"

"Okay, Barry. You go to bat for us, and I'll throw in the overnights."

"That's better, Rick, but you know what other incentive I need? I've become somewhat famous for it."

"That would be travel, Barry?" chimed in Terry.

"Well, what can you give me?"

"Do you ski?" I asked.

"Sure do. But it better be good!"

"I've connections with a first-class resort in Aspen."

"Nothing less than one week will do, Rick." *Sure. All of this with a low prime-time rate, huh?*

"I can arrange a package."

"My choice of dates?"

"Does that make it easy for you?"

"Okay. Your proposal is six thousand dollars per month, seventy-two thousand per year, *and* a trip to Aspen, right?"

"Yes," I confirmed. *I've got to be crazy, but this is another foundation account on the station . . .*

"Okay, I'll put you in the mix. Terry, give me a call early next week, and I'll let you know where we stand."

"Deal," said Terry, as if the deal was a go.

"Thanks, Barry," we said in unison, as we hung up the phone.

"You know we just gave away the farm," I said to Terry. "He's using our most in-demand inventory on our station and getting a trip. If this wasn't business we never had on the station before, I might have passed. However, overcoming the teen obstacle was difficult. You did a great job with the research. Now, let's close the deal. Send him a thank-you letter and an Aspen brochure that you can pick up at a travel agency."

"Got it."

The following week Barry called to tell me that we had lost the buy because of our teen content. I called Terry into my office.

"I just heard from Barry," I said.

"Give me some good news, Rick," he replied.

"We didn't make the buy."

"Why?"

"It was all about the teen content."

"I figured that would happen."

"Smart prediction."

"You know, Rick, anyone that wants to bleed us for prime day spots, free overnights, monthly promotions, and travel merchandise doesn't know our value."

"You're learning fast, Terry."

"Sure, but I would have loved to close a seventy-thousand-dollar deal."

"You'll make it up."

It was a learning moment for Terry. No matter how logical a deal might be, there's always a chance that you'll lose. Sometimes it doesn't make sense. And neither does sending clients on ski trips to Aspen.

Chapter 27

VICTORY TOUR

At the height of the Michael Jackson craze—he had recently hit a home run with the multimillion-seller *Thriller* album—the Jackson family put the band together for a final U.S. tour that was named the "Victory Tour." The tour sponsor, Pepsi-Cola, held the keys to a station promotion that would provide a sole radio outlet a premier promotional package—and the ratings leap that would be certain to follow—if it won the exclusive rights to the concert. Accordingly, Pepsi held onto hundreds of tickets and in-store supermarket contest rights. Since I-95 FM was a major supporter of Michael Jackson—"Billy Jean" was featured as part of the station's commercial soundtrack on television—we were determined to win the promotion away from Y100, the top-rated pop station at the time.

"We've got to find a way to win this promotion!" said Monique, our determined promotions manager at a hastily called promotions meeting. "There's no way that I'm going to allow Y100 to win this!"

The importance of the impending promotion had warranted the meeting's attendance by I-95's program director, Kenny Leonard, as well as Syd Stone, the general manager, and Benji Weinstein, the account executive on the Pepsi account. Monique was in a highly emotional state.

"Let's pull out all of the stops to earn this promotion from Pepsi," said Monique. "Since the concert is going to be held in Jacksonville, we need to gear all of our efforts to sending listeners to the show."

It was true. The closest location designated for the Victory Tour was Jacksonville, Florida, a five-hour car ride from Miami. The key would be to shuttle listeners to and from the concert, and there was agreement in the room that a bus caravan from Miami might be an option.

"I've got a better idea," said Monique. "Are you *really* ready to pull out all the stops on this once-in-a-lifetime promotion?"

"Here comes the money part. Let's hear it," said Syd. "You know how our newspaper parent company in Maine thinks about spending promo dollars. If they don't see a tangible return on investment, the likelihood of approving a big bucks concept will be slim."

"Well," offered Monique, "you're just going to have to get your big shoes on to make this pitch!" *Great . . . challenging Sid's ego just might work.*

"Okay," replied Syd, "let's hear it."

"Well, you know how I-95 has become famous for outsmarting Y100, right? Suppose we do something so crazy, so insane, so masterful that even Y100 couldn't possibly top it? How about chartering an airplane to fly listeners and key clients to Jacksonville?"

Silence filled the room as eyes opened wide.

"And how much will this cost?" inquired Syd.

"Let me get back to you with the figures, Syd. Kenny, let's discuss how we're going to give away tickets," added Monique. "We know that since the demand on concert tickets will far outweigh the available seating at the Jacksonville Bowl stadium, tickets will only be available by ordering them on an ad printed by the Jacksonville newspaper."

"So, how can we possibly have our South Florida listeners buy through a newspaper that's not available here?" asked Syd.

"Let me get back to you on that count, as well. I have a few ideas but want to button them down first."

"Okay, let me know when you've got the details together, Monique. Until then, let's keep this under wraps. No use allowing anyone other than this group to hear about it."

The meeting broke up. Monique motioned me to follow her into her office.

"Syd's really got his work cut out with the Portland management," she said. "I've got a lead on a possible charter, Northeastern Airlines, and have already placed a call to them. In the meantime, work with Benji and put together the best razzle-dazzle proposal for Pepsi. I'll do my part with Syd and Portland."

"Sure," I said, "just have a backup plan in case we don't have a blessing from corporate."

"No problem," replied Monique, "I've already got the figures."

"Get the airline rates nailed down, and I'll take them with me on the client presentation," I said. "I'm shooting to get a meeting with Pepsi as early as tomorrow."

"Okay. Stick around the office today. I'll need moral support for when he calls corporate."

I stood and returned to my office to find Benji standing in the doorway.

"Pepsi is waiting to hear from us," he said. "They've agreed to see us tomorrow but want to know if we can pass along any information today. I think we've got our competitor breathing down our neck. What's the latest?"

"Monique is working on getting information from an airline. I'm certain that Syd has already phoned corporate and put them on notice." It's just a waiting game. Why don't you put together a proposal that includes a fly-in to Jacksonville? How many tickets are they proposing to give us?"

"One hundred for their grocery promotion and an additional one hundred for our station–client giveaway."

"Let's ask them for another hundred. Our out-of-pocket is going to be huge, especially if we arrange to have *their* winners flown to Jacksonville on *our* charter."

Benji left my office, and I returned to the business at hand. My secretary, Barbara, appeared with a pile of messages in hand.

"What's going on?" she asked, "People are buzzing around here as if it's Christmas!"

"It is Christmas as far as I'm concerned. Benji will have a proposal for you to type in a few minutes. You'll understand why."

Later than day, my office phone rang. The flashing extension number was Monique's. I picked up the receiver.

"Ready for this?" she said.

"Uh-huh. . . . "

"Northeastern can do the charter. They want thirty thousand dollars."

"What? Are they crazy?"

"No, they say that's the going rate. No one else can touch this, Rick. I've already spoken to Kenny, and he's on board. We need to meet with Syd and help him with talking points for corporate.

"I'm on my way."

I hung up the phone and walked to Syd's office. Monique and Kenny were already seated, and I joined them. Monique was the first to talk.

"The best way to position this with corporate is to tell them that we are putting *all* of our rating book promotion dollars into this one contest."

"But we never promote the station during the summer months!" countered Syd.

"And a top-rated musical artist promotion never comes our way, regardless of the time of year," offered Kenny.

"Our business with Pepsi is very competitive, Syd," I added. "We are in a battle each time a buy comes down. This win will help us. We're talking twenty thousand for the promotion! Plus we're looking at grocery signs with our logo and an on-air promotion to give away tickets. Think of the benefits! It's only ten thousand dollars out of pocket if you look at it that way. And, think of the strategic position versus our competitor. You've always said that when it comes to beating them at their own game, it's job number one."

"Enough!" responded Syd. "I'm on your side. What's the on-air timetable, Kenny?"

"We can start immediately."

"Monique, can we pay half up front to Northeastern, and the other half once the last plane has landed back here?"

"Doubt it," offered Monique.

There was nothing left to discuss. It was up to Syd to sell the idea and expense to corporate as a one-time expenditure. He picked up the phone and dialed corporate.

"Jerry Jameson," said Syd into the receiver.

"Hi, Jerry. It's Syd Stone in Miami. How are you?"

Niceties over, Syd went into his pitch about the once-in-a-lifetime concert opportunity, on-air promotional, client involvement and contract, as well as the competitive benefits. He was practically out of his chair pitching it. We took turns looking at each other and at Syd. It was as if he was making an emotional summation to a jury, arms flailing and words spilling out over his desk. If we were going to get corporate's support, it was because of his fevered presentation. He finished up the call, took a deep breath, and hung up the receiver.

"Whew," said Monique. "I feel like applauding and coming around the desk to give you a big kiss, darling!"

"Not yet," replied Syd. "They aren't accustomed to one of their stations spending so much promotional money in so little time. Even though we've a budget for promotions, it would amount to adding to the dollars. Let's hope they move from their newspaper mentality to approve it. Now, go back to what you do best and let me handle this. I'll let you know when I hear back from them."

The remainder of the afternoon went smoothly. No difficult decisions to make. No drama among the sellers' clients. I had started to analyze my station inventory when Syd's secretary, Jayne, appeared in my doorway.

"Mr. Stone would like to see you." I stood and followed her to Syd's office. Monique and Kenny had settled into the same chairs as earlier.

"I heard back from corporate," offered Syd. "It's a go!"

We stood up in unison and applauded.

"Call Northeastern and have them send over a contract so that we can send it to corporate. An expenditure this large will need to be reviewed by the 'legal eagles' in Portland."

"Okay. I'll be in my office waiting for the final okay," offered Monique.

With the first step done, Monique summoned me into her office.

"We've got to act fast to get this on the air and beat Y100. Kenny has been listening to the station and heard that they are handing out a limited number of newspaper ad copies at their station tomorrow morning at ten a.m. You know the only way to get tickets is to fill out the application that is in the Jacksonville newspaper. How can we beat them at their own game?"

"I suggest that you work on a distribution other than via

our station, Monique," I replied. "I'll work on securing a news-paper from Jacksonville."

"And I've got a printer that will keep the presses going all night, if that's necessary, for us to have enough ready."

"That's great. Now let me get a newspaper."

I wondered if I might contact someone from the airline who flew from Jacksonville to Fort Lauderdale to send us a newspaper. It was approaching 6:00 p.m., and I was concerned that we needed to make certain that the newspaper was in Fort Lauderdale in time for us to get to the printer. I spent the next hour on the phone trying to arrange it. Miraculously, I was able to obtain the phone number and gate agent at Jack-sonville in time, as they were at the gate to board their 7 p.m. flight to Fort Lauderdale, the last flight of the day.

"Hi, this is Rick Charnack at I-95 radio in Miami," I said. "Is this Rob Dawson?"

"Yes, Rick, what can I do for you? I've got people in line checking in at my gate."

"I'm certain you know that the Jacksons are planning a concert in Jacksonville that is the sole location for their Victory Tour concert in the state. My station, I-95 FM, is *the* Michael Jackson station in Miami, and we're trying to get a jump on our competition and land a major promotion. You know that the only way to get tickets for the show is by sending in a form that is printed in the Jacksonville news-paper. If you can send me a copy of the newspaper on your next flight out, I will make certain you receive tickets to the concert."

"That sounds great, Rick, but I'm not certain I can get a copy this late in the day. They've been in short supply since the concert was announced. But I can try."

Rob assured me that if he could find someone to take over the gate check-in process, he would look for a newspaper and have a flight attendant bring it to us. Satisfied with his answer, I buzzed Monique.

"Put your printer on notice. I've got the gate agent for SkyAir trying to locate a newspaper that can be sent to us on the last flight out of Jacksonville. The flight arrives at 8:30 p.m., so we're going to have to act quickly."

"Okay, I've got it. And listen to this! While Y100 is offering a few newspapers at its station in Hollywood tomorrow morning at ten a.m., I've just arranged for all eleven Spin Records in Miami and Fort Lauderdale to have an unlimited supply of forms available when they open at the same time! We're going to beat them, Rick. We're going to beat them badly."

By all appearances, if all of the details worked out, I-95 FM was going to earn the Pepsi order by a long shot. Benji had already briefed his contact at Pepsi and secured at least the first one hundred tickets to be given away on the air. We still needed to convince him with a proposal for an additional one hundred for station guests and clients, as well as a contract for advertising on the station.

At 6:30 p.m., I phoned Rob Dawson, hoping for good news.

"I've been unable to find a newspaper," said Rob, "but I'm still looking. Don't lose hope!"

"Please, do your best. We've already set the wheels in motion hoping to receive a copy."

Rob assured me that if it could be done, he'd do it. I buzzed Monique and told her we were still on hold.

Finally, at 7 p.m., as the gate was about to close, I heard from Rob.

"I found a copy that has the coupon you're looking for. I'm sending it on the nine-thirty with Joan, our head flight attendant, who's been briefed and knows you'll be waiting at the gate."

"I can't thank you enough, Rob!"

"You already did, Rick. Remember the tickets you promised me?"

"Sure. You can count on it. Let me know where to send them."

After hanging up the phone, I ran over to Monique's office with the good news.

"A copy of the Jacksonville paper is headed our way on the next SkyAir flight!"

She was on her feet kissing me. "Amazing," she said. "I'll call our printer and tell him to warm up the presses."

"I'll meet you there."

Picking up the newspaper was akin to running a medley race and waiting for the baton. As promised, a copy of the newspaper arrived on the last flight. I drove to the printers and for the next four hours watched how the Victory Tour ad was clipped, readied for printing, and printed out. We ran five thousand copies to be circulated to the Spin Records stores. Monique had arranged for I-95's promotion team to drop off copies to the stores so that they would be available when the stores opened at the same time Y100 was handing out their handful of newspapers.

Our promotional announcements hit the airwaves at midnight. "We've got thousands of Jacksons ticket applications! Just stop by any Spin Records and pick up yours! And, make certain you stay tuned to I-95 FM. We've got more tickets to the show than any other radio station. Win yours by listening to I-95. Pass it on!"

Yes, this was the excitement that radio promotions were made of! It was more than just giving away tickets to the concert. It was beating our competition and savoring the results. In the end, our client came through with the additional tickets and a larger-than-expected one-month commercial order for $25,000! Our listeners and clients enjoyed our chartered jet to Jacksonville (especially the royal treatment of busses that pulled up on the tarmac to take them to the stadium).

It's a promotion that took the coordination of many I-95 FM staff and clients. I was amazed at how a team could come together and make something as important as a signature station promotion happen. To be part of a high-performance team was a feeling that I'll always remember. And one I'm certain our competition would prefer to forget.

AFTERWORD

L ooking in the mirror to shave, I could barely recognize myself. Underneath each eye were half-inch black lines that mimicked the polish worn by professional athletes. As I lathered up some shaving cream, my mind began to wander— thoughts of a simpler time when I first started in radio sales ran quickly through it. I had little more responsibility than managing myself and a list of customers in those days. Being a manager was simply a dream: a lofty goal that I had set for myself. And here I was, thirteen years later, having reached that goal and assembled a world-class sales team that was flourishing under my direction. How far I had come!

All of this success had come with a cost. It wasn't only my eyes that were showing the ill effects of my lifestyle. All of the partying had taken its toll on my body and, most importantly, my emotions. I had lost twenty pounds due to unhealthy eating and the consistent ingestion of large quantities of cocaine and alcohol.

With both hands shaking, I shaved, dried off, and walked to my kitchen. Glancing quickly into the living room, I noticed the mess left by the partygoers from the night before. Strewn over the coffee table were dusty remains of the party goods left over from what had been passed around the night before. Trivial Pursuit cards—a tradition during all-night parties—were scattered on the floor everywhere.

It was only partially clear to me (and my coworkers and family members) what my lifestyle had done to my emotional well-being. Arriving late at family functions, missing days at work, and manic mood swings had become the norm. I now harbored resentment toward the shallow, materialistic lifestyle all around me, even to those same rewards in my own life. To sum it up, I was spiraling out of control, and the heavy drinking and drugging to perform were no longer working.

On that fateful day, when I found it necessary to skip work because I was physically ill from what my body had endured the night before, my brother came to my apartment, unannounced, to discuss my ever-increasing problem. I admit that I was in denial and resistant to addressing my problem. In the mid-1980s, treatment for drugs and alcohol had yet to come into fashion. I pictured a facility where homeless drunks and heroin addicts—deadbeats who had been taken off the streets to protect themselves and others—were incarcerated. How could I, who lived on the eighteenth floor of a high-rise apartment building in full view of the ocean and was an overachieving professional, be subjected to the same treatment?

While it didn't all make sense at the time, I felt so emotionally spent that I was desperate—my negative thinking turned to an array of alternative thoughts and how it might be beneficial to spend time away from work and discover why I had chosen this path of self-destruction. It was a perfect time for an intervention. And so, on October 3, 1985, I entered the Care Unit of North Miami and commenced a twenty-eight-day treatment program.

As of this writing, twenty-eight years later, I am blessed with a life that's emotionally and spiritually far removed from my early days in radio sales and sales management. I no longer live for my next promotion in an industry that, even though I once loved it, took its toll on me. The irony is that it had created a Rick Charnack professional persona and delayed the discovery of who a healthy Rick Charnack was. You see, I had become a human "doing" for the benefit of a corporation and not a human "being."

Today I make decisions, without fear, often based on my intuition and not the impact on budget achievement. It's a life that I've chosen and not one that is necessary solely for financial survival. Yes, I've earned this opportunity to live my life more fully and am grateful for this chance to recant the experiences that brought me here. What a great relief!

My stories still amaze me—the fact that I could be successful on my own and lead others in an industry—and life— while using mind-altering chemicals. I now look back at these times with a wide variety of feelings: wonder, sadness, and even laughter!

To a large extent, they've made me who I am. And they've taken me on a path that I'll never regret.

ACKNOWLEDGMENTS

Fortunately, I had many supporters during my first writing project, and were it not for their kind words of encouragement, I'd still be wondering what to do with the next twenty years of my life.

These supporters include:

Dr. Vicki Panaccione, Nicole Arbalaez Lopez, and many friends and former associates (who remain anonymous) who contributed to the stories. Thanks to The Write Stuff Meetup Group who assisted in expanding my writing horizons, and to Ryan Collins for his excellent graphics and web expertise.

Thanks also to John Kahn, whose phone call to my home in Toms River, NJ, in 1972, set off a chain of events that ultimately led me back to Rhode Island and my first job in radio sales.

To my home away from home: Your Big Picture Café in Davie, FL, whose staff was always quick with a perfect latte; and to Carol and Gary Rosenberg, The Book Couple, whose feedback and expertise guided me throughout the editing, creative, and publishing process.

Most of all, I thank my brother, David, who helped me begin on this path; and to all my friends in recovery, who continue to reach out to those in need, encouraging them to live each day to the fullest.

ABOUT THE AUTHOR

Rick Charnack is a well-known and respected radio professional who has built a reputation for his creative approach to selling and marketing radio commercials and managing high performance sales teams.

He's consulted companies and conceived promotional programs for clients including Walt Disney World, Pepsico, British Airways, and Carnival Cruise Lines. His latest book, *RickRadio Confidential: Confessions of an Ad Man*, is a collection of real-life stories recounting his zany experiences in the radio business.

Rick currently resides near Hollywood, Florida, is single and spends his time writing. At any given moment, you might find him at Your Big Picture Café in Davie, FL, working on his first novel. He maintains a close relationship with hi daughter, Liza, who resides in New York City, and who Ric describes as, "the greatest gift of my life."

nce